Praise for *The Way of Valor*

"This nation was founded by entrepreneurs, so that's who will end up rescuing her from the Enemies of Freedom. Angie understands this and lays a path forward for loving parents who feel called to their ultimate purpose: protecting God's gifts to them. You will love this approach."

Sam Sorbo
Author, Filmmaker &
Education Freedom Advocate

"With her courageous faith and clear vision, Angie is on a mission to change education as we know it. *The Way of Valor* lays the groundwork for the rest of us to follow and provides a compelling path forward."

Dr. Lance Villers, Ed.D.
Superintendent, Santiam Christian School

"Angie Taylor takes her passion for Jesus and 30 years in education to create a model that helps students discover their divine destiny and add their unique value to the world. Her insightful approach to engaging students on a world-changing mission is truly inspiring! Every parent should read this book!"

Brooke Thomas
CEO & Founder, Live Out Loud

"*The Way of Valor* will inspire parents and educators to move past the status quo to envision a future for their children as creators, problem-solvers, and change makers. As a fellow professional educator, I heartily affirm her critique of current educational practices and her assessment of what is needed for change. This book will remind us of what's important about education, as well as highlight ways to move forward by going back to the essentials of what truly motivates us as human beings."

Deborah J. Miller, EdD
Author, Speaker & Educational Consultant

"*The Way of Valor* takes you off the beaten path of public and private education into the largely unexplored country of purpose-driven, authentic learning. I highly recommend it for anyone looking to be a change agent in K–12 education!"

Dr. Dennis Beck
Associate Professor of Educational Technology,
University of Arkansas

"Courageous educator, visionary, believer, fierce leader, and advocate for children, families, and communities . . . these are just a few of the things that come to mind when I think of Angie Taylor. I am thrilled she has penned this book to detail how to follow your dream, honor God, and establish a community that people are running to get into, instead of running to get out of. Perhaps most importantly, *The Way of Valor* shares how to RISE UP to the calling God has on each of our lives. I pray you are as inspired and emboldened by her story as I am, and that we put her ideas into practice to be the faith-filled leaders God has called us to be."

Julie Adams, MAT, NBCT
CEO, Keynote Speaker, Best-Selling Author & Educator

"Angie Taylor's contagious passion and global mission to have our children find their God-given purpose and strengths illuminates from the pages of her new book, *The Way of Valor.* This is a must read guidebook for every parent and educator looking to raise missional-minded and generous children. As a Valor parent and mental health professional, I strongly recommend Ms. Taylor's book as it's like attending the best parenting class ever!"

Dr. Mary Ellen Clifford
Psychologist, Manhattan Psychological Services

"Angie Taylor is leading a team of educators to come alongside our children, calling out their courage to dig deeper and dream bigger. *The Way of Valor* is an inspiration for families to raise up and lead with the truth and wisdom of Heaven. This book is a resource to begin shifting culture, encouraging and strengthening parents, and partnering education and families together to better our children."

Brittney Serpell
Loving on Purpose

MOVING STUDENTS FROM
APATHY TO *IMPACT*

THE WAY OF
VALOR

How a New
Movement in
Education is Raising
a Culture-Changing
Generation

**ANGIE
TAYLOR**

Published by

STORY ᯤ CHORUS

Dedication

I dedicate this book to my husband, Adam. His belief in me, along with his willingness to jump into the deep waters of big faith, has made this dream a reality. I will forever be grateful for you, my love.

Table of Contents

Imagine . . .

I write this book imagining unborn tomorrows.
Mark Batterson

Imagine a school whose staff understands that your child has a unique destiny . . .

Imagine a school where your student can be anywhere in the world, yet never miss a beat . . .

Imagine a school where parents and teachers effectively partner to raise world changers . . .

Imagine a school that moves students from entitlement and apathy to impact and contributing to the world . . .

Imagine a school where homework actually matters because it brings life-changing solutions to people in need . . .

Imagine a school that allows your family to be on a worthy mission while receiving a world-class education . . .

Imagine a school where your child has the opportunity to travel the world and make it their classroom . . .

Imagine a school where your child can choose any campus around the world to study . . .

Imagine a school where what your child learns actually prepares them for the world they'll face.

Welcome to Valor Global, where this school of our wildest imagination is becoming reality, because while we're the experts in education, parents are the experts in their children. And only by working together can your children achieve their full potential, fulfill their divine destiny, and make an eternal difference for Jesus Christ in this world.

So what does this really look like?

Allow me to introduce you to my friend Luke. He had a small challenge: donate or raise twenty-five dollars for a microloan that would help a life-changing business in a developing country. He discovered a hidden passion for helping others. And this homework assignment turned into a project called Loans That Change Lives, rallying dozens of people to support entrepreneurs in developing countries around the world.

Here's the fun part: Luke was an eleven-year-old student at the time.[1]

Luke took this assignment nearly a hundred times beyond what was required. Instead of giving $25, he raised thousands of dollars in just a week. This was about more than just getting a grade. He kept working into the summer and is still going, changing one life at a time with a goal of funding a hundred loans in countries across the world by the end of the year! Luke discovered that he could contribute to the world right now instead of waiting for when he grew up. And he did this while learning about business, different countries and cultures, analytical thinking, math and numbers, project management, and goal setting.

It's a near cliché to call our kids world changers. Because when it comes down to it, are they really? But Valor is founded on the premise that our kids genuinely can be, should be, and will be. All they need is an opportunity to contribute to the world in meaningful ways.

---

[1] Watch Luke Caro in action here: https://www.youtube.com/watch?v=Vgxmj8iL_Mw

Sounds amazing, right? Here's more great news: Luke is one of many Valor kids making a dent in the universe. I want to invite your family and community into this experience.

Think about the lost potential over the years as our education system has focused on stuffing content in, rather than drawing giftedness out. For us, education is about more than information—it's about transformation. We believe every person was created by God with a divine destiny and unique purpose. It's our responsibility to help them find their unique voice and learn how to use it. Our passion is to draw out their purpose and provide opportunities for students to fully realize their potential.

In this book I'll share our harrowing adventures through lush jungles and across African plains. I will introduce you to more remarkable kids like Luke, who bring clean water, electricity, and the miracle of education to thousands of children. And I'll pull back the curtain on how our world-class Valor Global team serves students and their families in more than forty states through our online school, as well as our brick-and-mortar campuses in Oregon and South Korea, and our sponsor schools in the Philippines, Haiti, Kenya, and Guatemala, every day.

We believe every person was created by God with a divine destiny and unique purpose.

But first, let me show you how it all began.

The System is Broken (and Everyone Knows It)

I started my education career in the public school system twenty-nine years ago at an inner-city Minneapolis school. I was a passionate follower of Jesus then, as I am now, and longed to introduce others to his extravagant love. I was fully committed to the idea that the world needed Christian teachers in the public school system. As image bearers of Christ we carry his light everywhere we go! However, the day I met a bright-eyed seven-year-old named Emanuel, I realized the system was not set up to help him succeed in life.

Emanuel was the youngest of nine children in a broken family battling drug addiction and more. Despite it all, his wit was sharp, and his mind was quick—though neither his grades nor standardized test scores reflected his brilliance. I only knew this about him from our personal interactions. This boy had divine potential, but the system wasn't cultivating it.

It killed me to see him be underserved, but even worse were the marks on his body. There was clearly frequent abuse in his home. Yet despite my consistent reporting of each new mark, nothing changed for him. Each passing week felt more hopeless. When I didn't think it could get worse, it did.

One morning Emanuel walked into class with a curling iron burn across his neck. This time it couldn't be hidden under long sleeves or pants. Emanuel also had a shaved head, so there was literally no way this was a silly accident caused by a child trying out a new hairstyle. When I asked him about this burn he said he tripped and fell, neck first, onto his mom's curling iron. But it was clear from the severity of the burn that it had been pressed against his skin, intentionally held there for some time.

At recess I marched to our school counselor's office and demanded we get him more help. Who was going to protect him from this abuse? The apathetic, overwhelmed counselor simply shrugged and said, "I believe his story about falling on the curling iron, Angie. I'll make a note of the burn and add it to his file."

This was my breaking point. A piece of paper shoved into a folder with dozens of other pieces of paper. That was the plan to help this bright, yet still-abused little boy.

I was stunned. How would anything change for this beautiful little boy?

I was overwhelmed. How could we help hundreds of other kids just like him?

I was changed. How was I going to make a difference, despite the badly broken education system that just kept getting worse?

I knew stuffing our kids with knowledge wasn't going to successfully carry kids like Emanuel through the brutal future that awaited them. I showed up to teach Emanuel how to add, subtract, and divide every day. But frankly, he couldn't absorb the knowledge because of the constant trauma at home. While Emanuel knew I loved him because I said it often, my love paled in the face of the awful things he endured outside of my classroom.

I had this little boy in my class for a year. Despite my best efforts, there was no way this short time would miraculously lift him from that traumatic pit. It was only the transforming power of an all-knowing Savior that could bring hope and deliverance for this child. When the year was over, it would be Jesus who would walk through the valley with him, not me.

As the year wore on, I realized more and more my inability to truly help my children prepare for the future they were being handed. At the same time, I fought tooth and nail with the all-powerful teachers' union. Even twenty-nine years ago the union was heavily involved in the political arena and had a clear agenda that was not simply about educating every child.

I heard from more than one leader in the union that their goal was to educate this generation without the values of Christianity. So there I was, facing off with an organization literally hell-bent on ripping our kids from the hope of heaven. I opted out of the teachers' union, which meant I had to pay *more money* out of my paycheck to not be in the union. It was madness! But no surprise, right?

Our union representative constantly badgered me, saying that even one accusation of wrongdoing would cost me my job. "You'll be alone," she said, "because no one is going to stand up for you."

At the same time, a curriculum designed to plant seeds of doubt into our kids about their sexuality and gender identities flooded into my classroom—and remember, this was nearly thirty years ago. What do you think it's like today? We were required to participate in pilot programs intended to drive a wedge between our children and Christian values, teaching ideas that parents may or may not have supported. Today, we're seeing the fruit of their work. It was pulled off so subtly that most parents were completely unaware of what was happening.

Subtly and stealth are tools of the enemy of our souls.

I longed to awaken children and their parents to the idea that they were formed uniquely, made with a plan and purpose in their mother's womb. I longed for children to understand that they were created in the image of the Almighty God. He makes no mistakes and creates no accidents. But in public education, my hands were tied. The system was rigged. And I believed there had to be a better way.

Eventually, through decades of working in private Christian education—which wasn't always that much better—I did find a better way. We call it the Way of Valor, which means personal bravery in the face of danger by partnering with God's purpose for us. We have five values that make our culture revolutionary in education.

WE BELIEVE OUR FAITH IS MADE COMPLETE AS WE TAKE COURAGEOUS ACTION. WE LIVE WITH GOD'S URGENCY AND PARTNER IN HIS GREAT RESCUE MISSION.

Our touchstone for every decision is this question: Is this God-honoring and Christ-centered?

If we genuinely want to resolve the issues today, and the thousands more that tomorrow will bring, we have to start with Christ. There is no justice without Jesus. Without humbly bending the knee at the level ground of the cross, we take on the role of either oppressor or oppressed, the judge or the accused. Reconciliation between people only comes with the gentleness and grace seen in Jesus. Education is a wonderful vehicle, but it will run empty before the finish line if we neglect the main thing: God's mission of a unique destiny for each person.

Being Christ-centered means recognizing we are eternal beings created for a divine purpose. This world isn't all there is. Jesus is the hope from today into forever. So we honor God by pointing to Jesus in everything we do. This means we will serve the least of these, build bridges to those who don't yet believe, and partner with God to set captives free.

Christ-centered means giving our kids hope strong enough to withstand the trials of life. When the best education in the world is simply not enough to withstand the intense storms life throws at them, their only hope to stay standing is found in the Gospel of Jesus. Jesus is the only one who commands the storm, "Peace, be still," and he is the only one the storms obey.

Christ-centered means being disruptors, not accepting the status quo handed to us. Jesus was brilliant and changed the world with twelve ordinary people. He didn't hang out in the temples waiting for people to come his way. He went out and transformed their lives. For this, Jesus was misunderstood. He was criticized and judged. Yet he held his ground, paying the greatest price for the truth.

Christ-centered means nurturing 360-degree health in our student's spiritual, physical, mental, emotional, and financial lives. Jesus showed us patterns of disciplined work and rejuvenating rest. He gave us the path to owning our unique identities while contributing to an eternal cause.

Christ-centered means embracing a new way of educating, thinking, and living. We follow the way of Jesus!

**WE ARE OBSESSED ABOUT BUILDING
A THRIVING COMMUNITY. OUR LIVES
ABSORB THE QUALITY OF THE PEOPLE
THAT SURROUND US.**

As the saying goes, we become like the five people we spend the most time with.

We're building an intentional community so our students can thrive together, building one another up. While parents have the greatest influence on their children, teachers and friends are tremendously influential as well. We understand that we all come to the table from different starting points. Some begin their journey with us as believers in Jesus, and others do not. What we all commit to is a culture of growth founded on a desire to seek more of what we were born to be. This isn't about sheltering our kids. Our goal is to create a vibrant community where they are prepared to meet the world with courageous faith and action.

While we have a strong online, remote learning model, we believe the data that tells us our kids need person-to-person connection more than ever. We have more opportunities to interact than ever before, yet we're dealing with the loneliest, most depressed generation in history. Almost 40 percent of high schoolers say they feel lonely and left out, a number that has increased even as they spend more time interacting online.[2] Community is key to thriving students and families.

Community is most powerful when it's not simply focused on itself. Our kids are capable of doing big things for others. So we provide them opportunities to create positive change together. If you join us, you commit to taking part in our cultural convictions and behaviors. This creates accountability and support when life gets hard.

A thriving community knows you at your worst, loves you anyway, and calls out to your divine potential.

A thriving community knows you at your worst, loves you anyway, and calls out to your divine potential. And isn't that the heart of Jesus? An effective, powerful community won't leave you where you are, because we believe you were meant for more than the status quo.

Valor is a community that sees, hears, and knows your children, so we can draw out their divine destiny.

[2]O'Donnell, Jayne. "Teens Aren't Socializing in the Real World and That's Making Them Super Lonely." USA Today. Gannett Satellite Information Network, March 20, 2019. https://www.usatoday.com/story/news/health/2019/03/20/teen-loneliness-social-media-cell-phones-suicide-isolation-gaming-cigna/3208845002/.

3

WE LEAD WITH COMPASSION AND LAY DOWN OUR WANTS TO BENEFIT OTHERS. GENEROSITY LEADS TO ABUNDANCE.

Compassion means *to suffer with*. We embody the heart of Jesus by fulfilling our biblical mandate of caring for the poor and needy. If Jesus's heart is broken, so is ours. Our strength is in our ability to help, give, and serve.

Compassion in action builds confidence because students understand they have the power to contribute in a meaningful way. If kids never do hard things, don't have an opportunity to try something uncomfortable, and never taste both success and failure, they become insecure. Their world grows smaller. Instead of stretching their limits and discovering they can contribute to the world, they compare each other on the basis of grades. They never find out their unique gifts were needed. Kids become insecure when we make the world about them.

Our students are vital to God's rescue mission on this planet, so we give them constant opportunities to improve the lives of others. This is the abundant path of Christ. This is where we find our own healing, gratitude, and significance. This is how we are made more like Jesus. As he said to the disciples, whatever we do for the least of these, we do for him.

We'll do everything in our power to provide opportunities for our students to encounter Jesus.

WE BUILD STUDENTS WHO ARE CONTRIBUTORS. CULTURE IS FORMED BY CREATORS, NOT CONSUMERS.

Culture is created upstream. The problem is, most children and adults live downstream, where they consume what others have created—generally for the worse.

Each of us was created with a divine destiny as unique as our fingerprints. However, our current education system was designed in the 1830s as a one-size-fits-all machine to prepare children to be factory and assembly-line workers. It squeezes exceptional children into a singular mold, regardless of their passions or skills. The goal of education today is to stuff content into heads, rather than to activate lifelong learners and innovators.

What if we started with the premise that regardless of academic ability or diagnoses, no child is broken, and instead embraced Psalm 139:13—that God knit each child in their mother's womb with a plan and purpose? Maybe the problem isn't with the students, but the molds we're educating them to fit.

At Valor, our job is to draw out the uniqueness in every student, teach them to gain confidence through competence, and help them navigate the ever-changing world successfully.

We also believe it's the creators, not consumers, who transform culture. Our students are becoming trendsetters, waymakers, and change bringers. We don't begin with a box for them to squeeze into. If we don't like the cultural trends we see today, we must develop kids who create the culture we want tomorrow.

5

WE BUILD CONFIDENCE BY COMPETENCE, PRACTICE, AND SUPPORT. OUR STUDENTS LEARN BOLDNESS THROUGH THEIR REAL-WORLD EXPERIENCES AND OUR BELIEF IN THEM.

Every student borrows from our belief in them.

We believe they were created with a divine destiny.

We believe they can make a positive impact on the world today.

We believe they are made to be leaders in an uncertain future.

We believe they will be most fulfilled when adding their unique value and contributing to others.

We believe they are more capable than they realize.

Personally, my mentors have given me the confidence to make the biggest, boldest decisions of my career. From moving my family across the country to lead a school I'd never visited, to cofounding Valor with the conviction that we can completely transform Christian education, my mentors have been the continual wind in my sails.

We can do this for our students.

The Way of Valor is For You If . . .

I wrote this book for parents who want to raise kids who contribute to the world in meaningful ways, and who also want to give them a way to practice making contributions today. Parents who know their children were made with a divine destiny to be awakened, nurtured, and guided. Parents who want a model with world-class education coupled with complete location flexibility.

Parents who want their children to have the opportunity to evaluate their faith for themselves, asking questions about their beliefs in a safe environment. Children need permission to see where their faith and culture agree and disagree, then have the freedom to explore these differences. We can trust that truth sets us free. When we seek Christ, we will find him. This is how we help children make their faith journey their own.

I also wrote this book for teachers who want to change the world, one student at a time. The teachers who are ready to embrace a radically different model of serving students because they see how broken and outdated our current system is. And the teachers who understand that students can impact our world right now, and that opportunities for global impact should be infused in our curriculum rather than confined to extracurriculars.

My friends, our opportunity to transform Christian education has never been greater. And the need has never been more urgent. I'm excited to have you along on this journey that is already changing lives in countries around the world—starting with your childrens'.

Welcome to *The Way of Valor*.

01

HOW KIDS WIN

"I don't have a building, and I don't have any money," I said, knees shaking as I looked out across the crowd. "But if you'd like to walk Jericho with me and believe God wants to use this dream to turn our kids from apathy to impact, enroll your children tonight."

It wasn't much of a sales pitch. Even though I was an experienced speaker, I was nervous that night in March of 2016. I'd been emailing friends about the vision I'd had for a school, sharing with them the ideas our team had come up with. I asked them to come if they were interested in learning more, and I was hopeful that at least ten people would show up.

Lord, even if only one comes, I'll be faithful to share the vision, I prayed.

The crowd overwhelmed the small sanctuary, many there to support me, a few there who didn't like me. But I went ahead and shared the dream of what was possible in education, laying out much of what you'll read in this book. That night, with no building and no money, eighty-five founding families paid to enroll their children and pledged to believe in God for the impossible.

Today, Valor is a special school. We have brick-and-mortar campuses in the United States, South Korea, and the Philippines. We have sister schools in Haiti, Kenya, and Guatemala, and an online campus, Valor Global Online. In all, we educate thousands of beautiful students. I can't wait to share more about all of them in the chapters ahead.

But one of our hallmarks as a school is that every student in our US, South Korean, and online campuses have an opportunity to take an international missions trip every year.

Some kids like to play it close to home by attending a trip in the US. That's wonderful because we do important work there. Others are a little more adventurous, choosing to serve our other students and their families and villages in places like the Philippines, Kenya, or Haiti. Each year we give the kids about a month to pray about where they want to go, because giving kids practice in seeking God's will for decisions in their life is imperative in their spiritual formation. Some are expensive and overseas in places they know nothing about, while others are a little "safer." It's up to students to raise their own money and take the initiative to make it happen.

A few years ago, one of our high school students named Rebecca felt called to go to India for her trip. The problem was that she didn't even like to go to friends' houses for sleepovers, much less spend a week overnight in a country halfway across the world! She was scared to go that far from home, and worse, she didn't think she could raise the money. It was well over $3,000, and her parents were unable to cut a check.

"I'm scared, Mrs. Taylor," she said to me, "and who would ever give me money for a trip like this? I can't do it."

She spoke softly, and her body language screamed defeat. I'd seen it a hundred times before. This was a kid who'd given up before the race started. Her mindset was fixed. The thought of going so far from home terrified her. She believed she couldn't do it—so what was the point?

I leaned in and made sure she met my eyes. "Rebecca, God provides for you where he's called you to go," I told her. "He knows your fear, and that's exactly why you need to do this."

She nodded and agreed nervously. She sure as heck didn't believe me. But I nudged her past learned helplessness, and her parents jumped in alongside her. We knew she could do it. All that was left was for her to realize it.

It was awesome to watch Rebecca's transformation as she took personal responsibility for God's guidance. And not only did she raise enough money for her trip, but she had extra that she gave to other students to help them with their trips. She was capable of more than she realized. But the story didn't stop there.

Once in India, in the heat and dust and all the activity, Rebecca became dehydrated and passed out, requiring a trip to the emergency room. I'll be real, standing over someone else's kid in an emergency room in the middle of India isn't something you want to have happen. And I thought, *Oh, great, this girl works her tail off to get here, and now this happens!*

A square of plastic sheeting hung from a white-painted bar to provide a little privacy between the beds, but it didn't do much to block out the noise or the heat of the day. Another concerned staff member from Valor stood nearby as we got plenty of fluids in her. Soon her color returned, and she sat up, responding to questions with a smile. Instead of being upset and shaken up, she was invigorated!

Rebecca's win was that by leaving her comfort zone, she experienced God's promises personally. Her faith became real. Her missions trip turned from a story of fear to one of overcoming, and how Jehovah-Jireh always provides. People can argue with you about a lot of things, but they can't argue against what you've experienced.

Creating prayer-filled, possibly risky, yet substantive experiences is what our kids need. We've had kids come to us, paralyzed with anxiety made worse by parents who are trying to protect them. These are kids like Rebecca who are afraid to stay a night away from home but end up taking multiple trips around the world to places where they meet God while doing hard things for him.

It's hard to watch kids face anxiety head-on, knowing they're afraid to fail, but also knowing you have to let them take that step anyway. We certainly keep them very safe and have rigorous protocols in place, like helping Rebecca get fluids before her situation grew complicated. But that didn't make it easy. This is how kids learn that it's OK to fail, which is the only thing that keeps them from playing it safe their entire lives. I've seen it happen hundreds of times for students, I've pored over the data that confirms it, but most compelling, I've lived it.

Personal Responsibility

You may call me crazy, but what if I told you that kids who flourish most embrace the phrase *personal responsibility*? Usually the only people concerned with responsibility are parents and educators. Kids couldn't care less. And if we're honest, we probably believe that most kids spend their waking hours trying to dodge responsibility.

As parents and teachers, we want to develop responsible kids so they can thrive as adults. But convincing a child to accept personal responsibility, much less embrace it, seems like a pipe dream. While I can't promise your child would ever put it on a T-shirt, I can share with you what happens when they take personal responsibility for key areas of life. It doesn't just change their lives—it changes entire families.

Researchers define responsibility in children as "the habit of choosing and accepting the consequences of the choice of behavior."[3] And its effect on kids is profound. In a landmark study, a group of fifth graders were given a series of tasks.[4] Some of them were solvable, others were impossible to complete. However, the researchers weren't interested in the kids' abilities. Instead, they were testing for attitude. The students who believed that effort, instead of ability, was most important to success solved the most problems. The researchers learned that these kids took personal responsibility for their work. On the other hand, the students who took less responsibility for their effort failed the most. In effect, those kids threw up their hands and said, "I'm not good at this, so I can't do it."

Psychologists call this learned helplessness. This is when someone faces difficult situations and stops trying to improve their circumstances—even when they actually have the power to do so. And it's not only found in kids. Adults struggle here as well. Psychologist Martin Seligman at the University of Pennsylvania dug into what learned helplessness does to people, young and old alike. Learned helplessness creates "the inability or unwillingness to act, including low self-esteem, chronic failure, sadness, and physical illness."[5]

The students who believed that effort, instead of ability, was most important to success solved the most problems.

[3]Mitton, Betty L., and Dale B. Harris. "The Development of Responsibility in Children." The Elementary School Journal, 54, no. 5 (1954): 268–77. Accessed August 1, 2021. http://www.jstor.org/stable/998563.

[4]Dweck, C. S., & Reppucci, N. D. (1973). Learned helplessness and reinforcement responsibility in children. Journal of Personality and Social Psychology, 25(1), 109–116. https://doi.org/10.1037/h0034248.

[5]Nolen, J. L., "Learned helplessness." Encyclopedia Britannica, December 28, 2017. https://www.britannica.com/science/learned-helplessness.

When we believe we can't do something, it stunts our growth, kills self-esteem, and breeds failure. Learned helplessness through a lack of personal responsibility is the norm in our society. Interestingly, a study found that the high school teachers most likely to blame parents and kids for low academic performance needed the most professional development and had the worst attitudes.[6] They didn't realize their blame game was showing up in the classroom and adversely affecting their ability to teach. Learned helplessness that sprouts in kids blooms in adults—even when we should know better.

Now, I have a hunch that you and I have the same goals for your children. We want to raise happy, healthy, well-educated kids who are gritty enough to roll up their sleeves and do hard things. And science shows us that the pathway to these goals is helping them take personal responsibility (while we do so ourselves). So the big question is, how do we do that? And in the modern educational system, *can* we actually pull that off? The answer is yes—but it takes a radically different approach to education.

Farewell to Comfort Zones

Valor almost didn't happen. In 2016, I was head of a highly ranked Christian school in Oregon. We had a waiting list from here to Timbuktu. Every week new families visited for tours, excited about their kids' possible futures at our school. Our standards were high, and our students' test scores were even higher.

[6]Thompson, Gail L., Susan Warren, and LaMesha Carter. "It's Not My Fault: Predicting High School Teachers Who Blame Parents and Students for Students' Low Achievement." The High School Journal 87, no. 3 (2004): 5–14. Accessed August 20, 2021. http://www.jstor.org/stable/40364292.

Our staff morale was high because we knew we were doing important work—and doing it well.

This kind of success had been my dream for nearly twenty-five years. Our school was killing it, and I had the extreme privilege of leading the charge. However, I'd met a major disruption to my plans: God was leading me to resign in the middle of the school year. It didn't make any sense from the outside (though I'll let you in on some difficult things that were going on behind-the-scenes later). People were shocked. Parents were upset. Some staff even felt betrayed. But instead of telling God this was too hard . . . too scary . . . and doesn't make sense . . . I knew I had to own His call and take responsibility for my level of obedience.

Two days into being jobless, I was writing in a journal to get my thoughts together. I wanted to figure out exactly what I now owned and what my actions would be. Where did I fit? What impact was I supposed to make? And where?

"My decision to resign was not about the school, or me, or my job," I wrote. "It's about building His kingdom and making His name great . . . It's about every person still sitting in their comfort zone."

Bam. There it was. I had to step outside of my comfort zone, and I desperately wanted to be part of helping others do so—especially students. Comfort zones are where natural talents and supernatural calling go to die. Comfort kills dreams by snuggling us up in a warm blanket, convincing us it's better to stay on the couch. It also kills our impact. Because our yes becomes other people's breakthroughs. And this is where Valor was born.

The next couple of months were miraculous, as we didn't just start one school, but two. However, I'm not the hero of the Valor story—God's miraculous call and provision are. And you are the one with the ability to make this book's message come to life by

Comfort zones are where natural talents and supernatural calling go to die.

partnering with this world-changing movement. You're the one with the ability to make this book's message come to life. And it takes disrupting your comfort zone.

How Do You Win?

Matthew was adopted as a young boy, and he came from circumstances that set everything against his chance for success. It seemed that his personal history would define his future as he made one bad decision after another. It wasn't just affecting him, but was disrupting others in the classroom to the point where they couldn't do their best work. As head of school, I was willing to work with students through any struggle, but I drew the line when choices impacted others.

I wanted to keep Matthew in school long enough to help him past this self-destructive point because I could see he was full of potential. The only way we were going to help him learn to make better decisions and grow up was to work with his parents. The truth is, for teachers, parents can be a scary thing. Matthew's parents never blamed the teachers or other students for his problems, but in my public and private school experience, that was extremely rare.

Beyond that, I know this firsthand because I'm a parent. I get it. I understand. My children have had their struggles too. When my son, Mason, would be involved in an "incident" and I'd ask what happened, inevitably he'd start by saying, "well, so-and-so did this—" and I would put up my hand.

"No," I would say. "Talk to me about what you did without using anyone else's name. You have to start this conversation with 'I,' because you are the only one you can control in this situation."

The home is ground zero for teaching our kids to take ownership and personal responsibility. I wanted my son to see that taking ownership starts even in the language we use to describe a situation, whether saying it out loud or even thinking about what happened. For my son, it was getting him to think according to ownership-inclined questions. What was *his* role? What did *he* do? Why did *he* do it? It doesn't matter what anyone else did.*

However, it's worse for everyone involved when parents take the opposite approach. Parents who didn't take ownership for what their kids were doing ended up with kids who didn't take ownership for their own behavior either. It's a vicious cycle. Remarkably, Matthew's parents had jumped right in to own and correct his disruptive behavior. This was an important step. And I'm happy to say Matthew course corrected and moved on.

His parents worked with us in every way, never allowing blame to be directed at any other student or staff at the school. Matthew was even required to write letters to his teachers taking responsibility for his behavior. Didn't do your homework? Own what you *will do* in the future in writing. Disrupted the class so other students couldn't concentrate? Own what you *will do* in writing.

Why all this effort? Why put the kid through all this? This was painstaking, not just for Matthew, but for the adults in his life who were methodically trying to teach him something very important about dealing with problems. We wanted him to understand that, before anything else, you first have to take ownership in your situation.

You can't be responsible for what isn't yours. You can't fix what you don't own. And you can't win in situations you decide you can't influence.

While I use Mason as an example throughout this book, I want to say that his father and I are so proud of the man he's become. That's why I can use him as an example at all—because he is godly, wise, and everything any parent could hope for!

My son is an excellent soccer player and played throughout his primary school years. But one year, he got little playing time. To him, this was horribly unjust. "Mom, I'm better than so many of the kids who play all the time!" he complained. "I don't get it. This coach just doesn't like me, and it isn't fair."

As a parent, it can be tempting to send an email or pick up the phone and get to the bottom of why our child (who's obviously God's gift to the world) isn't playing. However, I learned a simple and profoundly effective question to ask my kids in situations like this: How do you win?

So that's exactly what I asked him. He bristled and tried to explain how this was all the coach's fault. But because he's a huge history buff, I followed up with this angle: "What would a Spartan warrior do? How would they win this impossible situation?" That usually kicked him into overdrive, and he'd find a way to win.

You can't be responsible for what isn't yours. You can't fix what you don't own.

We talked it through, bit by bit. He realized he could simply ask the coach what he needed to do to get more playing time and help their team. So he did it, and it worked. I could empathize with the real emotions from a tough situation, responses that come from things that might be beyond my son's control. But the question that's in front of him is not how he feels, but how he wins.

You win by owning what you can and influencing it. Soccer is a simple example, but the mechanics are the same everywhere. What you own you can change, you can fix, you can claim, you can learn from, and you can find a way to win. Every situation, no matter how much it seems out of your control, has space for you to own something. And it's critical we teach our kids to take appropriate levels of personal responsibility.

Frustrated that your child is a benchwarmer in sports? Have them go to the coach and ask how they can earn playing time, and then have them be willing to do the work.

Upset that your child is still playing second violin? Maybe they need to put in more practice or rethink how they view the situation. As famed conductor Leonard Bernstein acknowledged, the most difficult instrument to play is second fiddle, because no one wants to do it.

Ownership of the situation looks different for each person, but going to the coach and demanding playing time is different than humbly asking what can be done to earn that time. Ownership finds a win not in the amount of playing time that results, nor in which orchestra chair you occupy, but in how you take control of your part of a situation and what you learned about yourself in that moment.

When you don't control what you should be owning, it can often control you. You lose. Everything becomes a temporary rental that'll get taken from you. You're like a ship without an anchor, at the mercy of the waves, always a victim with no control and no options, with no chance to meet goals.

It's kids like Matthew that have incredible potential, these disruptors who don't follow the rules and without a doubt have enough spark to change the world. But only if you can get them to take personal responsibility for their lives. They have a lot of energy; it simply needs to be pointed in the right direction.

Surprisingly, the worst thing we can do is to try to fix everything for our kids. For parents who are very concerned about protecting their kids, they say a lot of negative things to them. Much of it is unspoken, but the kids hear it.

"I don't believe you" is what you say when you talk over or around them to a teacher.

"You can't do this on your own" is what you say when you step in to handle a situation.

"You need someone to save you" is what you say when you come to their rescue.

"You can't handle hard things" is what you say when you don't insist your kids keep showing up even if something is difficult.

That doesn't build strong, independent kids. It creates insecurity. If we treat them that way, why are we surprised when they fail to mature into responsible adults capable of handling whatever the world throws at them?

How Do You Handle the Road?

Look out the closest window, and you'll see a Toyota drive by in no time. That wasn't always the case. After WWII, the Toyota Motor Company had a big problem: American auto manufacturers were lightyears ahead. They outproduced Japanese automakers and built better quality cars while they were at it. So the CEO of Toyota sent an engineer named Taiichi Ohno to the US to figure out how to catch up.[7]

Of all the things that inspired Ohno, supermarkets influenced him most. While it seems odd, he realized they were doing something right. Grocery stores had just enough inventory on hand to meet customer demand without stocking so much that food went to waste. This sparked an idea. What if they could reorganize their manufacturing process around eliminating waste? Instead of mass-producing every knob, bolt, and hubcap in advance, they could simply build the parts as needed.

[7] Kemp, Alex. "Taiichi Ohno: Hero of the Toyota Production System." QAD Blog, 5 Nov. 2020, https://www.qad.com/blog/2018/03/taiichi-ohno-toyota-production-system

In theory, this would mean lower wait times, eliminate over-production, simplify the assembly line, and more. Other managers didn't like the idea. Wouldn't they run out of parts? Wouldn't it slow everything down? Wouldn't they lose what precious ground they had gained against the Americans?

Turns out, no. And in fact, it wouldn't just increase their productivity by a degree or two. It transformed manufacturing forever. Today, this is known as *just-in-time*, or *lean, manufacturing*. And it's used by everyone from automakers to Silicon Valley tech startups. It may surprise you, but it's also made its way into Valor classrooms. Instead of manufacturing, we've applied it to the learning process.

Just-in-time learning treats every experience as a learning opportunity. Instead of knowledge stockpiled in our textbooks, we want the right information to be available when applicable. Learning takes place when knowledge is practiced and applied. We can either prepare the road for the child or the child for the road.

Most of that road is out of our control. And if you can't prepare a perfectly smooth road, you'd better make sure your child is able to handle every pothole or roadblock waiting for them just over the horizon.

Instead of developing anxiety over which curriculum or summer camp your kids need to get prepared, consider just-in-time learning.

This is the idea that every experience has a learning opportunity. Parents need to learn to ask themselves, What is the adult skill set I want my child to learn in this situation? Too often parents assume the teacher or the coach will handle teaching kids what they need to know, and the kids miss the opportunities that can prepare them for the road ahead.

When there's that kind of a disconnect between parent and school, a student who's doing poorly is a bit of a mystery. Are they capable but simply not trying? Or are they incapable and in need of some help?

A few years ago, I had a student who came to me after receiving a D and an F, wanting to see if he could do extra work during the summer to bring his grades up. I pulled up his file and quickly saw that he had made a valiant effort in one of his classes. He'd tried, he'd struggled, and he'd failed. The other class was a different story. I could see he barely opened his textbook.

"I want to honor your effort in one of your classes," I told him, and gave him some extra assignments to bring his grades up. "But in the other class, you're going to have to take the F."

What was the just-in-time lesson in that moment for that student? In life, always put in the effort.

Maybe a teacher really is the problem. Maybe the starting lineup isn't in your child's future. Instead of going after the teacher or blaming everything around the situation, the best thing you can do for your kid is to empower them to ask themselves: How do I win?

By refusing to teach our kids to take ownership of their lives and accept personal responsibility, we're directly to blame for the loss of human potential. The spark of brilliance you see in your child will soon be gone as they look around them for someone to blame for their failures, thinking they are justified in bad behavior.

Flat, paved roads carefully prepared by parents don't make for strong and capable adults. Bumpy roads that require effort to navigate create resilient, solutions-oriented adults.

My oldest daughter, Lauren, is a good example. Early on, she learned about ownership and personal responsibility in our home. When she got to college, she served with Habitat for Humanity. While in college, she dealt with quite a few unfair situations, as any college student will, yet she focused on working hard and finishing well.

When she got married, she and her husband made the choice to live in a modest apartment and made a point of saving money. This was about delayed gratification, an ability that's one of the best indicators of success but is lacking in kids who get to coast down the road instead of pedaling up the hill, avoiding potholes, to coast down the other side.

At age twenty-four, she met with a financial counselor, owning the decisions that would affect her financial future. She and her husband are now college-educated professionals, putting away money for a first house. Instead of complaining about student loans, spending money unnecessarily, and blaming others for her situation, she took extreme ownership of her life.

Part of taking ownership is learning to understand that your life has worth. If our kids only learn to deal with circumstances when they are dropped in their laps, they aren't being taught to think about future goals. They aren't thinking about what is worthy of their life, and what they should spend their life on. When kids don't learn to think about what their life is worth, they spend it chasing after a paycheck, possessions, and job titles.

Your Definitions Define You

How do you define success? The way you spend your life gives those around you a hint, even though most people have never actually thought about defining success. Maybe they've let some outside force define it for them, or are simply too busy chasing things that they believe are part of a successful life.

For my husband and I, being successful means that our family is growing in our relationship with Christ, and that we still gather every opportunity we get, because we are healthy with quality relationships. It means that our schedule is filled up with friends from all over the world. It means that we are able to give generously to organizations or people whenever we feel led by God to do so, without checking our bank account. It means that we look out the front window and see a beautiful countryside, not more houses. It means that we can travel whenever we want. It means that we can define our own goals instead of letting others do it for us. It doesn't mean a super expensive car or designer clothes or exclusive club memberships. There's nothing wrong with those things, but it's not how we define success in our lives.

If you don't know what success looks like, how do you know you're even on the right path? Most parents want their kids to be successful, but lacking a definition of success means you've created a vague goal that's impossible for them to achieve.

At one of our Valor family retreats, we encouraged people to create family creeds. "In this family, we stand for _____. In this family, we live by _____."

It was incredibly powerful, because the families came together and got on the same page. It defined success as a family and set up what it actually looked like.

"As a family, we decide to give our best."

"As a family, we decide to always choose the truth."

The creeds that came out of that retreat were incredible. What many parents thought was going to be a retreat for their kids turned out to be a life-changing event for entire households.

Part of that was because we were intentional about coaching parents and giving them the space and time to work with their kids. One of the main things we coached them on was how to handle moments where, in the past, they've done nothing at all.

I had one mom who loved how Chip and Joanna Gaines had a holder for each family member's cell phones so that no one would use their phone at the table.

"You could do that," I suggested. "My kids aren't allowed to have phones at the table."

If you don't know what success looks like, how do you know you're even on the right path?

"Oh, my boys would never do that," she said. "They refuse to put their phones away at the table."

"Do you pay the cell phone bill?"

"Oh, they'd never talk to me!"

"They will when they're hungry," I said.

Parents, you're modeling behavior for your kids. You need to own the situation so you can take control. It's awful at first, but you have to stay the course. Consistency over time has a compound effect. Help your kids know that yes, you can, and you will.

If you don't start now, you may never start.

Personal Responsibility, Educator Style

Parents aren't the only ones who need to take personal responsibility for the good of their kids. Teachers have to do it too. When a student fails a test, it's the teacher's personal responsibility to ask whether they are capable of passing. You have data points to know if they were.

If they aren't capable, you have the responsibility to make some changes to help them learn the material better. But if they were capable? Your personal responsibility at that point isn't to coddle them, but to connect with them and their parents and be direct.

"You were capable of passing this test. What's up?"

From there, you have two choices: What would be the better learning experience? Making sure the student knows the important material, or letting them take the F? Either way, when a student gets an F, they'll learn they need to try harder, study more, or come to the teacher and ask for a chance to bring their grade up.

I was a teacher with large class sizes, and I absolutely understand a lot of teachers are overwhelmed with red tape and handouts and grades and policies. I know how exhausting it can be to teach a large class. But teachers have to own the feedback loop.

Slow things down. Adjust the learning process so kids grasp valuable information and understand where they were and weren't successful and why. Keep parents in the loop instead of avoiding them out of fear they're going to be difficult.

Clearing a way for a student to grow means making sure you've removed every barrier you have ownership over. Keep parents involved. Talk to the student. Constantly assess their ability. Encourage self-advocacy. Because ownership without self-advocacy is only a partial win.

Owning your part in a situation without pushing for the opportunity to change it leads to a shame spiral. One of the most important lessons kids take into college, marriage, careers, and health is the ability to advocate for themselves.

The student who got the D and F advocated for himself. He asked if there was something he could do to improve his grades. But what if he'd had his parents come talk to me instead? Maybe the grade outcome would have been the same, but he'd have never learned he could handle it on his own. When kids think you're coming to save them, they'll never advocate for themselves. Self-advocacy only grows out of personal responsibility. It's a complete loop.

We must give kids opportunities to practice both personal responsibility and self-advocacy before adulthood. As parents and educators, we can't expect that once they turn eighteen, kids will magically be able to take responsibility for themselves if they haven't been practicing.

We started this book with personal responsibility because it's the linchpin for success. Instead of enabling students into learned helplessness, we empower them to effect change in their own lives. They learn that they're powerful, capable, and self-determined. They don't need to exist as blame shifters and victims of a system beyond their influence. As parents, we need to partner with our child's future self and their teachers to help them along—but we also need to embrace it for ourselves!

Personal responsibility is caught as much as taught. Rebecca experienced this in India, but only because her parents gave her enough rope to run with. Personally, I experienced this starting Valor in 2016. As both a teacher and a parent, this is the single most important and challenging lesson we can learn ourselves and pass on to our children. But it is so worth it.

Learned helplessness is the default mode of today's consumer-driven culture and of the classrooms it's infecting. School teachers and parents alike are held in its grip. It's killing self-worth, personal growth, and the results our children achieve.

But it doesn't have to be this way for our students.

I knew that if things were going to change for kids—mine, yours, and every kid around the world—the Valor team had to take personal responsibility by really asking how we did education and being willing to disrupt it in a big way.

Valor partners with parents and shows kids using just-in-time learning that they are capable of more than they ever thought possible, preparing them for a challenging world instead of trying to remove the hard stuff. Our future is filled with problems we can't even fathom today. So it's going to take a resilient, gritty, and creative generation who know they're capable of handling anything life throws at them.

02

BEGIN WITH ETERNITY IN MIND

Our current education system focuses on the content, not the learner. It's all about cramming information in instead of drawing their destiny out. There's a huge difference between seeing a human being as something to inform instead of as someone to help transform. "But they need to know this stuff!" might be the reply as we load up their backpacks and brains with facts and data, measuring how well they retain it all. The system is so focused on testing results and creating informed students that we forget to consider if what we're doing will actually help them when the big storms of life come along.

"You're carrying lots of information," the system tells our kids. "Somewhere in there is probably enough to get you through on your own."

Will massive amounts of information give our kids hope? Will it help them fight their way out of a dark place? If our kids think it's only themselves against the world, using their own smarts built on prepackaged information, they're in trouble. We have to start with the end in mind and ask ourselves how to partner with the future of this child.

Independence Is Built on Interdependence

While we value freedom at Valor, we also value interdependence; we are working across many cultures all around the globe. One of the dangers of telling Westerners to embrace freedom is that we confuse it with individual rights and forget what freedom looks like in light of the community God created us for. In 2005, researchers studied the responses of people from Western nations and East Asian nations as they looked at an image of a tiger standing in front of a jungle background. Westerners focused on the tiger, while Asians focused on the jungle.[8] In our culture, personal freedom and agency is prized, while in many Eastern cultures, community and connectedness to the whole is more valued. Both are important in raising a whole and healthy child.

Freedom and personal agency can exist in a healthy community. They are not mutually exclusive. Think of Starbucks, which is found all around the world. You go into one when you're traveling, and you'll see there are some commonalities. The drink menu is mostly the same as what you're used to. The ambiance and branding are the same, but the language is specific to the country. If you've just spent the afternoon sweating in the heat and humidity of Buenos Aires, walking through row after row at La Recoleta Cemetery, it's nice to know that the nearby Starbucks will have a cold drink and a restroom. You can bank on what you know about Starbucks, and in that way, there is a thread of sameness no matter where you are. Starbucks has built a model based on a foundation of those customer expectations all around the world.

Freedom and personal agency can exist in a healthy community. They are not mutually exclusive.

---

[8]*Merali, Zeeya. "Westerners and Easterners See the World Differently." New Scientist. New Scientist, August 22, 2005. https://www.newscientist.com/article/dn7882-westerners-and-easterners-see-the-world-differently/.*

The independence pops up in the pastry case. That's where you realize you're in a different country. From quesitos in Puerto Rico, to choux cream bread in South Korea, to sufganiyot in Israel, the pastry case is not the same as what you'd see in a Starbucks in Anywhere, USA. Within the interdependent structure of Starbucks, there is room for pastries that reflect the local culture and community. Their strong business model is a foundation that allows for freedom to exist on top of it.

Early in my education career, I had a boss who was a brilliant leader of a private school. But he made it clear that he ran the school, and that we were there to make his ideas happen. There was no freedom to do anything of our own adaptation, no matter the situation. Today as Valor continues to grow, that private school is shrinking because there is no room for ideas from the community. "My way or the highway" doesn't allow for that meshing of independence on top of interdependence. Yet the early church model we see in scripture was one where they had free agency to choose to support those in need. We don't just share our resources, we also share our dreams and ideas. I know that independence built on interdependence works, not because of Starbucks, but because of Valor's own origin story.

Jeff Ahn and Sarah Byon are cofounders of Valor Global Foundation and were a huge part in starting the first Valor school in Portland, Oregon. Jeff has master's degrees from Columbia and is working on one at Harvard. He has been leading the Valor school in South Korea, and has been also instrumental in leading the school in the Philippines. How he got there is quite a story.

Jeff comes from a Korean-Chinese background, though he was born in the US. He lived in Korea, China, and Japan, moving around the entire world and living with different family members. Eventually he and his brother moved with their grandparents from Korea to the US.

He moved back to South Korea and started an afterschool SAT academy, but he felt that God wanted him to do something else. He came back to Portland, Oregon to help his nephew find a school he could attend when he moved to the US. It was at that point that I met him.

He came in for an interview at the school I was a principal of, and as we were talking, he shared his vision for a Christian global school. I listened as the very same ideas I'd been thinking and sharing with others were validated through his voice. Here was someone who lived on the other side of the world, with the same God-breathed idea I had about education. Within twenty minutes, I knew we needed to work together.

"I don't know why, but I think we should work together," I said. "Your ideas for a global school are exactly what I've envisioned."

Jeff was taken aback and thought I was a bit crazy. He didn't have many American friends yet and had barely started to converse with me, and yet here I was, asking him to partner with what would become the Valor project.

"I really think we should work together," I pressed. "It doesn't matter if you're in Korea. I feel like God wants us to work together."

It would never have happened if he hadn't been willing to share his dream, and that's why it's important that you speak your dream out often. We were both brave enough to share our preposterous dreams with each other, which is very much a way of Valor. I had to look a bit like a lunatic to Jeff, asking an almost complete stranger if he'd like to work with me. But it became an example of that interdependence that stretched across the globe.

Jeff introduced me to Sarah Byon, who had very big dreams of building God's kingdom along with us. Some things we did to start Valor were done in the US, while other things, such as the website design and the promotional materials, were designed by Sarah and made in Korea. The schools are interconnected—relying on, thriving alongside, and learning from each other—built on the same foundation but with their own unique qualities, just like the Starbucks pastry case.

Our current education system confuses self-focus with independence and creates future disasters in the lives of our kids. We think we're creating strong and knowledgeable humans, capable of acting as powerful lone agents, when what we're really doing is dissolving necessary community and interdependence they'll need to survive.

When we become all about ourselves with no community, there is no mission. There is no greater purpose. And there is no hope that you're going to make it through the storm. Everything we need to thrive as human beings and disciples of Christ is destroyed in a self-focused, information-gathering education system. You know how I know this?

I look around.

Wherever I see institutions focus inward, pushing the message that merely being informed and feeling empowered is enough to go it alone, I see them dying. I see people floundering. I see confusion. Whether it's a church or a school, a lack of any kind of outward focus is a symptom that inspiration has left the building long ago.

Margaret Mead said it best: never doubt that a small group of thoughtful, committed citizens can change the world. Had I stayed quiet at my kitchen table, trying to create this school on my own, it would have failed. We had a big, global vision that would take all of us, a community, to accomplish. Families and staff helped provide the momentum and energy to see the vision through.

AN ARMY OF ONE HAS ALREADY LOST

No one makes it on their own. We all need something that calls us to push at a harder level. If we're going it alone, who's there to help push, and who's there to cheer us as we reach our goals?

People who aren't moving atrophy very quickly, whether it's physically, mentally, or spiritually. When there's nothing inspiring us onward and upward, we become complacent. After that, we start to feel worthless. Then daily life becomes mindless and pointless. We pursue shallow things and shut down everything we need to help us crawl out of the pit when we find ourselves in such places. We think the pit is all there is, and there's no hope.

We might be informed, but we were never transformed. We're stuck.

Everyone is going to have bad experiences in life, but transformed people handle it differently. They know how to work their muscles and get out. They know there's more to life than what's happening right now.

They know they have a tomorrow because they know they have a divine destiny.

Believers in Jesus Christ have a divine destiny, and it's one you can only find when you're in a relationship with your Creator. And because you have a Creator, you know you were created for a purpose. This is important, because sooner or later, every person asks themself what life is all about.

If it's all about you, you've already lost.

Finding fulfillment is going to be impossible, and you'll look all over before you realize that nothing satisfies, not even trying to fulfill what others want from us.

Imagine being the third-generation son of a family that has owned and run a store in town for generations. The name of the

If it's all about you, you've already lost.

store even includes "and sons" on its sign. There's no question what your future is expected to be.

If it's what you want to do, wonderful.

If it's what your parents want you to do, they're seeking fulfillment through you.

Parents fulfilling their dreams and living vicariously through their children isn't a new story, but it is a heavy one, because God's intention for us is directly connected to the desires he's placed in our hearts, not what others desire for us from their heart.

But if you haven't been transformed and are traipsing through life with a broken definition of independence, you'll let others define fulfillment. We never quite get that our frustrating life is directly tied to ignoring the desires God put in our hearts.

Solomon is the best example of this. He was the richest, wisest man on earth, whose wisdom came directly from God. He had any and every thing he wanted, and people traveled from far away to see his wealth and wisdom in action. He was also the author of Ecclesiastes, a book in which a majority of its verses painfully explores the meaning in life.

"We're locked in an endless cycle. There's nothing new under the sun. We just forget everything that already happened and do it again. Everything is meaningless, meaningless . . ." he wrote. But by the end of the book, he came to a final conclusion. "Fear God. Work hard. Fulfill your purpose. Enjoy your life."

Marching to someone else's drumbeat is how the living die a little bit each day.

LIVING WITHOUT PURPOSE IS ACTUALLY DYING

Self-focused living is purpose-free living, and it's how people atrophy and die.

Consider the conundrum of early retirement. That's supposed to be the pinnacle of success and fulfillment, being able to retire from the rat race as soon as you're able so you can start relaxing and enjoying your life.

Except it really doesn't work that way. Studies show that men who retire early die earlier than men who retire at age sixty-five or older.[9] A 2016 study found that healthy people who waited a year past sixty-five to retire had an 11 percent lower mortality risk.[10] Even unhealthy retirees who waited a year past sixty-five lowered their mortality risk by nine percent compared to those who retired sooner.

Who knew leisurely golfing and sleeping in every day could kill you? In the wrong hands, retirement can lead to day after day of meaninglessness, an Ecclesiastes 2.0, with no reason to get out of bed and no purpose to accomplish.

We were created to work, and fulfilling work is found when we acknowledge what our Creator has put in our heart. It's not something you created or conjured up inside. It's not something someone else can put in you, whether that's a parent or a celebrity. It's something your Creator, who knows you the best, put in you so you can let it come out, instead of you focusing inwardly on self.

It's your destiny.

[9]Waldron, Hilary. "Social Security Administration." *Social Security Administration Research, Statistics, and Policy Analysis*, 1 July 2002, https://www.ssa.gov/policy/docs/workingpapers/wp97.html.

[10]Brenoff, Ann. "Early Retirement May Be the Kiss of Death, Study Finds." *HuffPost*, HuffPost, 28 Apr. 2016, https://www.huffpost.com/entry/early-retirement-may-be-the-kiss-of-death-study-finds_n_57221aa3e4b01a5ebde49eff.

Experiencing Transcendent Purpose That Lasts

Ever get home from running errands and realize you can't even remember the drive? You picked up the dry cleaning and got the groceries but don't recall much of it.

Most of us operate in a default state every day, unconsciously making decisions. There's a place for that when you're running errands, but not when you're living the broad scope of your life.

You have to transcend thoughtless, typical existence and connect with your Creator who has a good plan and purpose for you.

You have to transcend thoughtless, typical existence and connect with your Creator who has a good plan and purpose for you.

Transcendence is when you experience life or a moment beyond the normal or physical level. We pick up cues on what's considered normal by what happens around us, calculating an average of what people are doing and saying. It's not a great idea to let others determine what's normal, especially if you're using that to feed your autopilot. But if you've been on autopilot a long time, it's hard to grasp anything else.

Pastor and author Mark Batterson has a great exercise where you create a timeline of your life, writing every significant moment down. It doesn't matter what you put down, or even if you understand why something is significant enough to add to the list. The goal is to simply write down everything that comes to mind to you as significant.

Then you pull back and look at it. What's the common thread? What stands out?

When I did this exercise, I saw that I was consistently leading and disrupting the status quo. I was either calling someone
or something out or trying to get to a higher spot than where I
was at.

The next question in the exercise is: What venue does this
play out in?

It might seem odd, but as an educator, I don't read many education books anymore. I read leadership books. If you understand
leadership, you can equip your students to do everything. But
without the benefit of the timeline exercise, I'd found it confusing
that I wasn't reading the "normal" books I should be reading. I
didn't even like going to teacher development and all the standard activities I was supposed to enjoy and find fulfilling as an
educator. Something was off-kilter; I wasn't wanting to do the
things a person like me should want to be doing.

It's unsettling to not feel fulfilled by the things I was told I
ought to be fulfilled by. I didn't fully break free from allowing
outsiders to define what fulfillment was until I went to India
in 2013.

As a country, India is one of the most exhilarating, exhausting places I've ever been, full of sights, sounds, and warm-hearted
people whom I love. There's not a moment when sensory overload
doesn't overwhelm you. The smell of the sewers draining into the
streets mixed with the exhausts of vehicles rushing by; vehicles
which apparently had no traffic laws to obey. The perpetual dull
roar of horns, street vendors, and an endless sea of people. Throw
in the cows, camels, and elephants meandering about, and it was
pure bedlam.

But then there's the beauty. The gorgeous fabrics with rich
colors and intricate designs, delicate bits of fringe and metal

beads at the edges. The scents of amazing spices and food wafting in the air, making you hungry when you hadn't thought you were. The beautiful people and unique culture that draws you in.

The experience was one of constant cognitive dissonance. Nothing about it, from the sensory overload to the mix of scents, cacophony, and music, made sense.

I had twelve students with me on that missions trip, and we were all exhausted and jetlagged. Trying to take it all in to understand what was happening around us was overwhelming, though we had ample time to give it a try as we rode a bus for hours, working our way out to a church in the bush.

The church only had a roof with poles holding it up. The pastor had one page torn out of a Bible to use, and he'd read the scripture to the hundreds of people who had walked from all around the region. They'd recite it back to him three or four times.

Despite not having many translators, they wanted us to pray for them. The thing that blew my mind was their faith and spiritual hunger; it was so strong that you could almost feel it. When they'd ask me for prayer, The Holy Spirit led me to exactly what they needed prayer for, even though I couldn't understand their language. When an older lady came to me for prayer, God told me to put my hand on her side. The entire team prayed like this for those needing healing, for those needing to be set free—it was incredible to watch God show up in our prayers. And as we watched them heal, they encouraged our faith.

Three of the boys who were on spiritual fire, praying during that night of healing, had experienced God move in their lives just a day earlier. These were three teenagers who, if anything would happen on the trip that would get us in trouble, I was sure it would come from them. The night before the healing service, these three decided to climb up on the roof, breaking every rule we'd told them. I don't know what they had planned, but God was waiting.

"Maybe we should pray," one of them said at one point.

They opened their mouths to pray, and the Holy Spirit dropped in like a heavy wind, pushing them to the roof. When they tried to get up, they fell back down. All they could do was pray. The next day, tired and bedraggled, they told me what happened.

With the experience of the healing service and what happened with these boys, I had an epiphany. First, we have to get out of the way and give kids the opportunity to encounter God directly. Second, I finally realized what desire God had placed in my heart and how I'd find fulfillment. Whatever form it did or didn't take, whatever route God led me on, my goal was to spend my life helping people get access to God's word.

WE ARE ONLY FULFILLED WHEN WE'RE OPERATING IN OUR DIVINE PURPOSE

God intersects threads he's been weaving in our lives all along. I had been a fan of Sir Ken Robinson, who wrote about getting kids into their passion and element to help them find their purpose. His words were already in my mind when this all happened in India, which helped me make the connections.

Our divine purpose leverages the gifts and experiences God gives us.

He has his hands on our lives, and he doesn't disconnect them when we finally latch onto our divine purpose. My gifting and experience was all in education, and I knew this was where I would apply what I had learned.

In America, our main desire is to create comfortable, happy kids, which often means we end up blocking what God wants to do. It's not uncommon for parents to pull their kids out of Valor

Our divine purpose leverages the gifts and experiences God gives us.

around ninth grade so they can have a "normal" public high school experience. Over time, I watched the fires lit through experiences like the missions trip to India fizzle and slowly die. "Normal" experiences don't feed the furnace, they dampen it. Even the kids who'd had intense experiences firsthand struggled, back in their comfort zone of regular life and low expectation.

We're losing our Christian kids because we've lost a sense of urgency and replaced it with comfort and safety or a desire for them to have "normal" experiences. It wasn't enough for me to instill urgency in my own kids; I wanted to do it for others' kids as well.

After India, everyone was required to go on a missions trip. If you were too young to go, you were involved in some other way. We had second graders raising money for mattresses for our orphans in Haiti so that everyone had ownership in what was happening.

You keep the fire lit by raising the standard and calling out the best in others, because people rise up to meet it. God created us to be part of a community, to contribute our voice to the world, to fulfil the purpose burning inside. You can see this drive in people today as activism increases. It's simply a question of who is doing the driving, whether it's God or the world.

By requiring missions trips, we saw massive shifts in our students. Remember Pig Pen, from the Peanuts comic? We had a kid like that. He was tall and a little awkward and didn't do well at school. On his home turf in America, he was like a clutch with stripped gears. Nothing was catching. But then he went to Mexico on a missions trip, and all the gears caught. For the first time, he fit in. He was contributing in a meaningful and significant way.

I watched him go from misfit into a workhorse, a servant like nobody's business. It was amazing to see, and I almost wanted to leave him there because he had blossomed. It was a beautiful example of how you help kids unlock their divine potential when you provide opportunities.

But what if you stuck him in a traditional school structure? What if you locked him into a "normal" experience? He would've been taught to memorize information and that he only mattered if he got As. Get a D or an F, and you don't matter because you're dumb. Achieve as we tell you to achieve, or you don't amount to anything.

Traditional school structures start with the wrong premise. We absolutely must start from the premise that each child has a divine creator. If someone has dyslexia or Down syndrome, they're not broken; we as educators just need to understand how to teach them in the way they can learn. We all matter. And it's the educator's job to help each one flourish. It's the educator's job to help each one experience long-lasting, transcendent purpose.

Starting From a Blank Page

"When engaged in battle, the slightest flinch may determine the outcome . . ." I wrote in my journal in 2016. I had learned this truth over the years, and it's a good thing I did; I love troublemakers because I see their potential, not their current trouble. They're my favorite. Frankly, they are world changers just testing their wings.

Sitting across from me in my office one afternoon was just such a student. Michael wasn't new to my office and quickly assumed a slouched position in the chair, arms crossed, giving me attitude as he spoke, every possible way he could.

After listening to this for a bit, I interrupted. "I'm going to shove what you said aside for the moment and ignore it," I said. I reached into a drawer and pulled out a piece of paper, sliding it across the desk toward him.

Michael looked at the paper, then at me.

"Write down everything you want me to believe is true about you," I said. "You have a blank page. What are you going to fill it with?"

He seemed taken aback. "I don't know," he said.

"'I don't know' isn't a thinking answer. If *you* don't know, we're in trouble."

He didn't respond, though he did sit up a bit.

"Let's use myself as an example," I said. "I'd want you to think I was a godly woman, that I genuinely loved my students. What is it that you want people to believe is true about you?"

He reached for the paper and began writing. *Honest. Hard worker. Smart.* He wrote faster.

What inevitably happens in these moments is that I never have to go over the specifics of the incident that sent a student to my office. Instead of some defensive dance where we get lost in the details and blame, something else happens: they expect a lecture, they don't get it, and they open up on their own.

They start talking about it themselves, and I point to what they want to see in themselves, written in their own handwriting on the paper. We talk about how to get there, what goals need to be set, and I ask them how I can help.

I do this with kids all the time, and it's one of the most powerful practices I do as a principal. And not once in all the times I've used this technique have I had a student write down that they wanted me to think they were a lazy, lying punk.

Michael isn't the only one who's visited my office in hot water. We had a brilliant eighth grade student, Will, who single-handedly hacked our online grading system and curriculum. He had a lot of fun assigning bogus quizzes and work to other students, as well as giving some of them As. It was a confusing mess when it was all done.

When Will came into my office, I could tell he was terrified. He came from a culture where shame was a strong motivator, and things looked pretty bad for him, both in school and when he got home.

"Hey," I told him. "I have to be honest. I literally want to high-five you right now, because that was a brilliant hack."

He looked a little surprised, but also wary of whatever hammer was going to drop next.

"Seriously, I wish I'd thought of hiring you to test our system for vulnerability," I said. "Yeah, you shouldn't be writing quizzes for students, but the hack was amazing."

That got the conversation going. We talked some more about ways we could give him room to use his power for good, and years later, his college entrance essay was about what happened there in my office.

I could've seen Michael as a mouthy punk and Will as a troublemaker who made a mess of the computer system, thinking they both deserved to be suspended and nothing more. But I could see that their destiny was wrapped up in the skill sets that got them into trouble. It's imperative that we stop telling kids what *not* to do, and instead start calling out to their divine potential and partnering with the future of that child.

It took me a while to learn that truth, though.

Spencer, Alek, and Anthony were three students from a Christian school where I had been the principal. I was friends with their parents, and they were great Christian kids, except for their continued problem of getting into trouble. They simply did not fit into the traditional school mold, and it caused issues.

One day they all ended up in my office for the final time.

"Spencer, the problem is that you don't think before you act," I said. "You have to pause and think before you take action." As a young and inexperienced principal, I was at my wit's end.

Fast forward to August 2015. I was on social media, scrolling through the news, when I began reading about a terrorist attack on a train to Paris. I read about the courageous efforts of three young Americans, along with four other passengers, who subdued a heavily armed terrorist.

No way. Are you kidding me? I thought when I read the names. There they were—Spencer, Alek, and Anthony, the three boys from that school.

They were heroes.

I read how Spencer charged at the gunman, and then winced a bit at his reply to the reporter, who had asked what was going through his mind when he did it.

"Nothing," he said. "I didn't think before I acted."

Thank God he didn't get what I tried to drill into him. I'd failed at how I'd handled those boys in school, trying to wrestle the "trouble" out of them when it wasn't the problem at all. I should have been identifying their gifts, calling to their divine potential.

How dare we categorize kids by how well they follow our rules? How dare we discount someone God has made? How dare we question his design and try to reshape it to find a different, more manageable mold? God knew that day on the train was coming, and he knew how many lives needed to be saved. He made those boys to be action-driven, and I was glad I failed to change that.

Kids are like wild horses. Our education system tries to break them so they can be controlled instead of asking how we can harness and direct their energy to something good. The blank page, that clean slate, is an opportunity to awaken that transcendent quality they were born with, that divine potential that every child has, buried under the label of troublemaker or dumb or failure.

Please don't misunderstand me. There is a time for discipline. However, that's meant to help a child develop into their future rather than simply punish them in that moment. At Valor, we ask the question of whether this will help the kids develop in the way needed for their future or if it will simply break them. Every child has divine potential. They just need help seeing it, and this is our starting point at Valor.

03

RAISE UP CREATORS

Are you too far down the river? Author and leadership coach Dan Heath shared an analogy in his book *Upstream: The Quest to Solve Problems Before They Happen.* It goes something like this:

You and a friend are having a picnic alongside a river. It's a beautiful sunny afternoon, and you're enjoying companionable silence while taking in the beauty of nature. Suddenly, your relaxing day is interrupted by a shout for help coming from the direction of the water. You realize a child is drowning, and without thinking, you both drop your sandwiches and dive in.

You grab the child and swim to shore. But before you can recover, you hear another child cry for help. Once again, you and your friend jump back into the river to rescue them too.

Then another struggling child drifts by . . . and another . . . and another. The two of you can barely keep up with all of the drowning children. Out of the blue, you see your friend wading out of the water, apparently leaving you alone and exhausted to continue the rescue effort.

"Where are you going?" you yell as your friend walks away.

"I'm going upstream to tackle the guy who's throwing all these kids in the water."

Despite your good intentions, you've been solving the wrong problem all along. Sure, kids drowning in a river is a problem, but it isn't *the* problem. The real problem is located somewhere else, farther upstream.

Real solutions only come when we are able to identify the real problem. When you put all your energy into solving the wrong problem, you'll never stop having problems to solve. Our education system does a poor job teaching kids to deal with problems; they take a firm downstream approach, both in how they work with kids and how they teach them to handle the world.

"Here is a problem," our education system tells our kids every day. "Your job is to tell me if the solution is answer A, B, or C."

Real solutions only come when we are able to identify the real problem.

There's no creative thinking involved in being told what needs solving and selecting from a limited set of solutions. This gets to the heart of what it means to be a creator: someone who doesn't sit around waiting to be told what the problem is, but is instead a problem finder.

You're not looking for trouble, but neither are you surprised (or incapable) when you find it.

The Creator's Manifesto

True creators innovate. They develop meaningful solutions that serve humanity. This is at odds with how we've defined creators today, though, because we have a lot of meaningless innovation being heralded as life-changing when it really isn't. We cheer every bit of generic creativity where no problem is solved and the quality isn't even that great.

"You reinvented the wheel! Fantastic! Good job!"

"You invented an app that solves a problem no one knew they had nor desired to fix! Excellent work."

Creation that solves no real problem and does nothing for humanity is chaff in the wind. The true creator's manifesto keeps a few things in mind.

POSITION YOURSELF TO WIN

At Valor, our development team spent many nights identifying the problems in education and brainstorming solutions to these. We wanted to acknowledge the current reality of education. We knew that partnership with our parents was going to be the key to success in our schools and for kids. Remember how I said it's important to ask how you can find the win in whatever situation you're in? When something is dropped in my lap that I have zero interest in dealing with, something I don't like at all, I'm still empowered to win.

Do I need to work harder? Learn in a different way? What's the root issue? I'm never going to win if I'm fixated on the symptoms instead of the problem itself. I also have to have a firm belief that I'm designed to win, to overcome, and to add value to the world. Creators are positioned to win because they can identify the actual problem and create solutions, no matter what the situation is.

BE WILLING TO SERVE

The serving mindset is what most people skip when it comes to creativity. That's unfortunate because selfish creation usually creates more problems than it solves. Selfish creation is all about looking out for number one, with a goal of notoriety or wealth instead of service.

○ ○ ○

Creators are positioned to win because they can identify the actual problem and create solutions, no matter what the situation is.

We've worked hard to teach our kids at Valor the value of serving.

We start by helping them realize that people are basically the same no matter where you go in the world. Cultures vary, but our problems end up being similar. However, sometimes our students have a hard time understanding that other countries aren't like the US. The same problems can't be solved the same way; it depends where you are. Creativity based in hearts genuinely wanting to serve can still miss the mark if they don't understand the real problem.

As you'll see, we've helped create solar power solutions and water purification systems in other countries, but we've learned the hard way that if you don't do it in collaboration with the people there, it's a disaster. You have to first ask them what problems they identify, and then what resources they have that we can use to help solve the problem. Part of serving is true listening.

If you go about it any other way, you end up with mountains of donated clothes they didn't need, or bucket irrigation systems that don't work.

DEFINE THE PROBLEM YOU'RE TRYING TO SOLVE

It's hard to answer a question you haven't asked, yet it's amazing how many people leap to problem solving before they even know what the problem really is.

When you want to get to New York City quickly, you don't hop on the first train in the station without making sure it's headed to New York. Don't mistake movement for solution; there's a time factor involved in all viable solutions. Albert Einstein has a famous quote that if he "had an hour to solve a problem, I'd spend fifty-five minutes thinking about the problem and five minutes thinking about solutions."

Take the time to define. Brainstorm with your group, interview people, and figure out what's really the issue. True successful and long-lasting innovation comes from spending 90 percent of your time defining and understanding the problem that needs solving.[11] The scrapheap of failed ideas is full of poorly defined problems and a rush to solutions.

Valor has regularly hosted think tanks for parents, students, and staff, events where every voice matters. As we develop our schools, we adapt quickly to what we hear is (or isn't) effective.

MAKE MEANINGFUL, INTENTIONAL INNOVATION AND CREATION

"I'm just tossing ideas out there" makes real problem solvers shudder. It's a random approach to what should be intentional. A lack of solution usually isn't due to a lack of ideas, because ideas aren't rare. You can practically pluck them out of the sky. It's a truly innovative idea that gets to the heart of the problem that's hard to come by.

Intentional and meaningful solutions involve more than just educating people about a problem. We have lots of influencers and activists who do a great job at drawing attention to problems, but then they leave it hanging without a solution. Sometimes they try to cover it by saying they're merely bringing awareness. But is awareness of a problem without an offered solution useful in the long run?

---

[11]Staff, The Build Network. "You Cannot Solve What You Don't Understand." Inc.com, Inc., 9 May 2013, https://www.inc.com/thebuildnetwork/you-cannot-solve-what-you-dont-understand.html

Some people are very good at identifying the problem, and some people are very good at coming up with ideas, but you have to do both to accomplish anything.

KNOW YOU HAVE A UNIQUE CONTRIBUTION TO MAKE TO THE WORLD

Each of us has a unique lens and voice through which we can add value back to the world. It's easy to sit back and say, "I'm not important, and what I have to say doesn't matter," so that you're never on the hook for finding creative solutions. That's the mindset of a consumer, and it's hard to add value when you're busy consuming instead of contributing. If you get the serving part of creativity right, this shouldn't be a problem.

Creativity has the power to embolden kids, but we wonder why they lack self-esteem. The reason is that we've turned them into consumers, and instead of uniquely contributing to the world, they're trying to be knockoffs. They weren't born to be someone else, but we've created a world that tells them they should be.

My cofounders in the online school, Doug and Thea Wood, saw a significant problem in education. They had their kids in a very expensive private Christian school. One year they took their children to Israel. When they returned, they discovered that the school was more concerned about missing assigned homework and that their children had missed too many days in school.

The Wood's had given their children an amazing journey to the Holy Land, something very valuable in the life of a believer, but there was a disconnect with how the school saw education. The Woods could have come up with a solution for their family only, but they took personal responsibility to solve it for others as well by cofounding Valor.

Seeing the World as It Could Be

Do you see what is, or do you see what could be? Creators see the world as an endless possibility instead of closed and finite, a living thing that can be moved in different directions. Because of this, the content they create dictates the culture. They have a long, endless view of what can be done, and that pushes the culture along.

Consumers, on the other hand, allow culture to be dictated to them.

They look around, see the world as it is, and accept it. They have zero hands on the rudder and are at the mercy of going where the creators tell them to go. They take on the identity they're told to take on, and they're more prone to complaining about, mocking, or destroying what others have created because they don't have firsthand experience in creating much at all, including their own future. Creators have all the power.

What did we teach our kids to be? Consumers, of course. We give them devices to stare at so they can consume images and information. We tell them to read a chapter in a history book and then answer the five questions. I had a teacher who came to me and told me that a student had copied his homework from an online source. It was true, and while the student shouldn't have done that, I saw a different problem.

"Your homework is flawed," I said to the teacher. She'd created homework that was geared toward consumerist behavior. "If you don't want them to copy work from someplace else, you have to create an assignment unique to that individual student."

We give them homework where they can copy and paste the answers from somewhere else. We tell them to consume the information, then spit it back out, and we reward them for their accuracy.

On the flip side, we punish creativity. In high school, resourcefulness and collaboration are called cheating. Coloring or behaving outside the lines is bad behavior. Nonconformity to rules or trends is disobedience, even though nothing new is created when everyone conforms.

As well-meaning as it is, we're basically sending our kids all the wrong messages. We're seriously dishonoring our kids by wasting their time teaching them to consume content they can find in a two-second internet search instead of creating. They never learn to look at problems around them with an eye toward finding a solution that will help humanity. Instead, we teach them to let the problems define them. At best, they muster up a reaction and live a life always on defense. Instead of raising kids who solve problems, we raise kids who can only react to them, completely at the mercy of outside forces.

SOLVING FOR N IN THE REAL WORLD

"Why do I have to learn algebra?! I'll never need it!" said pretty much every kid ever.

When we teach things like algebra in a consumer fashion, it becomes completely isolated from problem solving in the real world. If you're not going to be a math teacher, who cares about quadratic equations? Who cares about formulas and the order of operation? Consumer-based education is compartmentalized, and it doesn't translate well to real life.

We had a teacher who understood the value of algebra who, in the midst of teaching about statistics and ratios, decided to show her students how it applied to real life. She had them create a survey about something they were interested in, and then sent them out to do interviews based on their survey. Using the data they gathered, they did a statistical analysis to come to a conclusion.

"What did you learn about the world around you?" she asked them after they had finished the assignment. "What findings did you arrive at?"

There were some interesting answers, but the most telling was from a ninth grader who discovered an important truth. "I can get the results to say whatever I want by the way I ask the question."

That's a kid who is going to understand the world we live in very well.

So when are we ever going to use algebra in life? Every day when we watch the news or read something online. Every day when we're presented with information trying to persuade us to come to a specific conclusion.

Homework that can be copied is homework that doesn't require any engagement, and you can't create anything of value if you're disengaged.

The Problem of Problems

Imagine you're in a room with Agatha Christie. It's evening, the curtains are drawn, and rain is pounding against the glass. The fire in the fireplace crackles and flickers as she weaves a mystery, her voice lowering in suspense before growing in expectation, everyone edges toward the front of their seat trying to figure out whodunit . . . and then some guy with the CliffsNotes version hops in and announces the summary.

We do this to our kids all the time.

Problems are like a mystery to be solved, especially when it's a problem you've never faced before. As adults, we recognize the problem faster than our kids do because we've been there and done that. So we summarize the problem for them and completely rob them of the opportunity to learn to ask the right questions

Problems are like a mystery to be solved, especially when it's a problem you've never faced before.

and to figure it out on their own. Maybe we protect them from some pain for a while, but in real life, no one is going to tell them what the problem is.

We could learn a lot from the scientific method, which relies on first being able to define the problem before you have any chance of making legitimate discoveries. And to get to that definition, you have to ask a lot of questions.

My husband is great at solving tech problems because he approaches it methodically.

"I'm getting this random error message," I say.

"It's not random."

"No, it just pops up whenever," I insist.

"It's not random. Something is causing it."

And then he methodically asks questions and works through scenarios that narrow down the field of potential culprits until he gets to the real problem. You can solve a problem easily if you can define it, but "random" problems have no definition and are impossible to solve.

When faced with a problem, we either have the ability to ask the right questions and figure out how to define the problem, or we just stare at a random impossibility that will never be solved no matter how much time and money we throw at it.

TONGKO, A VILLAGE JUST FOUR HOURS FROM MANILA

When you see the Philippines from the air, it looks as if God just finished painting it with a wide, green brush, and the paint is still wet. There are darker jungles broken up by patches of brilliant green rice terraces and delicate palm trees surrounding villages.

The densely populated city of Manila, tucked into a bay on the west side of the island of Luzon, juts out above the greenery as a city of glass skyscrapers surrounded by a sprawl of buildings and crowded, bustling streets.

Slums trail out and around the city proper, and as we approached the airport on a missions trip, I was reminded that poverty looks remarkably similar everywhere in the world. That's because poverty is a mindset, not a geographic location. It's earmarked by garbage strewn everywhere and a general lack of stewardship. Whether you're in India or Haiti or Nicaragua, the amount of garbage takes your breath away. It's a problem.

About four hours southeast of Manila, on the other side of the large Laguna Lake, is Tongko. A river runs through the village, framed by small huts clustered near its banks, with a bridge spanning the water where mothers would do their laundry while their children played next to them.

We stayed in the small city of Lucina and took a thirty-minute bus ride to the trailhead that led to Tongko, where we hiked into the village to help a Korean missionary. The task wasn't small. There was one building without walls, open to all the elements. And for the most part, the village was unchurched. They'd send their kids on Sundays, but the adults didn't come. The missionary worked with the high school kids, calling them the disciples.

We quickly assessed the problem. They needed to have lights at night, which we decided could be solved through solar power. They also needed clean water.

We went to work and got a solar power and lighting system set up. We installed water filtration systems. The people in the village were excited, the missionary was excited, and we thought we were doing amazing things.

We came back a year later, excited to see their progress. What we found was that no one was using the water filtration system, the kids' teeth were rotting out, and the solar system didn't work anymore because the batteries had died.

We brought an American solution to a Filipino problem, setting up systems for them that they didn't have the resources to fix when broken. Even worse, we'd never asked them what they wanted. This time we decided to interview them to find out who they were as individuals and what they needed.

We asked them what their dream was for their kids. We asked how much money they made. We asked them what they thought their number one need was. We asked them if there was a way to make money so there could be an economic flywheel in the community. We asked them what resources they had available.

We discovered that they still needed clean drinking water, but first they had to understand that it was the bad water that was making them sick and rotting their teeth. They hadn't understood the problem before, so our solution for them was meaningless. We also learned what resources we had to work with and what they would be able to maintain using those limited resources.

It was a matter of education and understanding the need. Instead of preparing a solution for the village without asking, we changed our method. Now, five years into helping, it's a different picture.

It started with taking the village on field trips to Manila. Here was a village of people who had no idea that a world-class city even existed just four hours away. Most had never left their village and had no idea of much of the outside world's cultures. We certainly hadn't thought field trips would solve any problems, but we treated them as ways to acquire new information and enlarge their perspective. The shift in the people was dramatic and led to some specific changes.

Today they have lights. Our kids solved this problem after a year of research in their science classes and labs, using tin and water bottles that contained bleach. The bleach kept the water clear, and we placed the bottles in holes in the roofs. During the day, the sun shone through the bottle and functioned like a bright light in the dark huts. At night, small solar lights attached to the bottom of the water bottle, which had been charging all day, kicked in.

Today they have clean drinking water. The people in the village needed more education about why the tree filters were important, so our kids created storybooks that explained why filtered water was better. To combat high illiteracy rates that are common in the Philippines, they even did puppet shows for the adults. And yes, we changed the filtration system to one that was easier for the people to manage. But the most important component in this piece of the puzzle was bringing education to help them understand the need for the solution.

Today they are developing an economy. Students are teaching their parents to read. Buildings for new school rooms and a church are being constructed.

One thing we've learned is that education can help move the needle, but the number one goal to improve people's lives is growing the gross domestic product (GDP).

Since we have been collaborating with this village through one-on-one sponsorships, some of those teenagers (the disciples) were able to go to college. They have internet access, and we Zoom with them once a week to pray. All this because our students go to Valor and are engaged in adding value to the world.

If you can effectively define a problem, you can create a solution. If you can create a solution, you can monetize it. If you can monetize it, you will grow the GDP. And that's the best indicator that people will be lifted out of poverty.

How do you think our students felt about all the homework that went toward solving the light problem and educating people about water safety once they realized it mattered?

It's not the algebra or science that the kids hate, it's the inability to see that it matters.

It's not the algebra or science that the kids hate, it's the inability to see that it matters. They brought light into dark homes, helped little kids keep their teeth, and stopped moms from getting sick. When we connect their homework to something that matters, something they care about, they work tirelessly.

Design Thinking

Design thinking is a way to crash up against your assumptions about a problem and see if those assumptions fail. You want to start with a well-defined problem.

You know you've failed to define a problem correctly when the solution ends up being a convoluted, barely functioning mess. The solution acts like a mirror, and if all you see in it is chaos, you need to revisit your definition of the problem.

Feedback loops are a way to keep problem solving on track, functioning like the guardrails on the path. They force you to revisit your solutions to make sure they're still holding.

Unfortunately, we don't do any of this well in education. Kids get a paper with an A or F, and there's not much else for them to glean from it other than seeing their effort in comparison with others.

Education also tends to fail at the feedback loop when it comes to parents. Somewhere we got the idea that teachers are the experts on the kids instead of the parents. At Valor, we don't just say we're in partnership with parents so we can toss around a nice slogan. We actually listen to their feedback on what's happening with their kids so we can find out what the pain points are in the trenches. In a way, the school we have now has been built by students and parents through this feedback loop, and will continue to be.

Feedback loops don't survive well in the wild, though. They don't self-generate. Unless you build them into your system and maintain their use, they simply won't exist.

Take standardized testing as a classic example. It would seem like a feedback loop, since the theory is that it's testing kids to see where they're at. I give you a standardized test in April, and then in June, I send out all the reports that the test generated.

Do I care what those results are? Not really. I can't use that information to impact the students because they're moving on to the next school year. The most I can do is pass it on to the next teacher. And what do those tests tell us anyway? Maybe the kid with the high score is just really good at memorizing information or had a teacher that did a great job preparing them for the test.

One of the reasons we at Valor update different data points throughout the year, starting at the beginning of the year and onward, is that it helps the teachers understand who the learner is and what's really going on. We have StrengthsFinder tests, personality tests, and Measures of Academic Progress (MAP) tests with the goal of getting some context on who this student really is and what direction they're headed. This is the same reason we go back to the same villages year after year, because it helps us stay consistently informed so we know what's working and what isn't.

And that's why if you visited Tongko today, you'd find something remarkable.

You'd see electrical wires leading into the village. You'd hear the sound of hammers and saws from new buildings constantly being built. You'd see smiles of children without rotten teeth, their parents and siblings much healthier. You'd see kids teaching their parents to read, students who are proud to wear a uniform and attend school. Instead of a rough trail, there's a well-lit paved path leading not only to Tongko, but spreading out like a web many miles to the surrounding villages so that travel during the rainy season is possible.

Creative problem solving with consistent feedback is how we create paths that take us to wonderful, even unexpected places. Literal paths in dense jungles to pathways of wisdom in the classroom.

The Path of Wisdom

Our work in the world always parallels what we learn in the classroom. This is why we say wisdom creates paths, not positions. Our students were presented with an important problem and diligently worked to solve it. Through painstaking research, trial and error, and thousands of sketches in beat-up notebooks, they discovered a solution. Notice how different this approach is from rote memorization alone.

Instead of offering the solution and testing for recall, and then pretending that equals comprehension, we point them at the problem and ask our students to figure it out. This is what creators do—and it's how everything we see around us began.

In the beginning, God created. It's the first thing we learn about God, that he was a creator. We also learn that wisdom begins with fear of God.

When two women came to Solomon laying claim to the same baby and demanding he find a solution, he didn't take a position. He took a path, one that would reveal the truth.

"Cut the baby in two," he said.

One woman smirked. The other woman was horrified. It wasn't difficult to see who the real mother was.

The best lesson we get from Solomon is that the most important thing we should ask of God, who created us, is to give us wisdom.

Wisdom listens carefully with a desire to serve humanity rather than an ideology. Wisdom goes out and takes part in transforming action.

Wisdom leaves a well-lit path in its wake, a path littered with defeated problems, a path with a future. Wisdom creates paths to walk, ask, and explore, rather than offering a position students aren't allowed to deviate from. Wisdom is the rocket fuel of curiosity, exploration, and true learning—it is knowledge applied. Now let's turn to what this looks like every day outside of jungles and villages.

Wisdom listens carefully with a desire to serve humanity rather than an ideology. Wisdom goes out and takes part in transforming action.

04

WISDOM CREATES PATHS

The woman was standing over a tiny, round grill, cooking up the last tortillas and tucking a bit of rice into them. Her face was red from the heat. The sun was relentless, and as I put my hand up to shield my eyes, looking down the line of over a hundred hungry kids, I didn't know how to tell them that we'd run out of food.

We'd come to the slums of Tijuana to help a married couple whose ministry was feeding the children and sharing the Gospel. They had three children of their own and lived in the slum themselves. They were literally feeding their neighbors and relying on the help of Christian organizations to help them buy food to feed the children one meal per day.

These kids had stood in line, under the hot sun, waiting for a small meal. And they wouldn't get one. Thinking like an American, I motioned to the woman. "Where's the store? We have money, and I can get some more food."

She shook her head. There wasn't a store nearby. "They understand," she said, motioning to the kids in line. "They know if they want to get food, they have to line up early."

I was sobbing as I walked to where our team's bus was parked. Inside were the lunches we'd packed for the day. I pulled out what I found, dried my tears, and chopped up sandwiches, trying to have my own five-loaves-and-two-fishes moment. This was their one meal for this one day. And that was all we could do for them at that moment.

Tijuana is the city that marks where Latin America ends, the slums sprawling out until they hit the hard line of the US border. It's one of the fastest growing cities in Mexico and home to one of the world's busiest land crossings between two nations. Traveling between Earth and Mars would be about as easy for those who are trapped in the slums of Tijuana. Shanty houses crowd onto hills and into canyons, some peppered up the hillside while others are at the bottom, susceptible to terrible flooding when the rains come. Watery ditches along the dusty roads are choked with sewage and garbage.

From a distance, the homes seem to be stacked on top of each other. Construction waste from San Diego finds new life in Tijuana, as houses are built out of what is being thrown away in the north. Bright colors break up the rusty browns and weathered grays, splashed across the sides of buildings and carts and buses.

Heat rises with the dust, filling the air with the smells of smoke, food, and dank water. The noise of traffic is mixed with Latin music and barking dogs. Tires are splayed out like dark donuts, holding pieced roofs together, as reddish-tan dirt roads wind their way through the slums, sometimes serving as the only indicator that what are along the road are homes and not piles of discarded sheet metal and lumber.

In the midst of all this, we ran out of food.

We came back the next year to the same slum. Our goal was to set up a pantry for this couple's ministry, so everybody's suitcase was stuffed with food that we were essentially smuggling in, hoping to keep it from being confiscated or taxed at the border. We'd been collecting food for four months in California and didn't want to see it disappear before we got to Tijuana.

When we arrived, we had a surprise waiting. The woman who ran the ministry was just going into labor with the couple's fourth child, but before heading to the hospital, she insisted that she see and pray over the food we'd brought.

The baby died at the hospital.

Despite all the food we'd brought, there was tragedy. The whole team was in shock at the change from one day to the next.

"We don't have any money," the father told us when he and his other three children came back from the hospital. "We have to pay the hospital and bury the baby, and we don't have the money to do that."

We thought we'd come to the rescue, bringing a mountain of food and solving the problem we had come to solve, but instead everyone was crying. There was a much deeper need here.

I pulled the team into another room. "What do you want to do?"

"Why don't we give them the Disneyland money?" a student asked.

We'd planned a trip to Disneyland on the way back from Tijuana, and our kids had saved up money to cover the cost. It was a good chunk of change. I looked around at my team. "Is that what you all want to do?"

When you position kids to show up in the world in powerful ways, they'll exceed your expectations every time.

Every single student said yes. They wanted all the Disneyland money to pay for the cost of the hospital and burial of the baby. My heart was simultaneously breaking from the loss of the child while exploding with joy from my students. When you position kids to show up in the world in powerful ways, they'll exceed your expectations every time. They were experiencing what the Bible talks about when it says we are to bind up the broken-hearted. "Blessed are the poor in spirit" was no longer just a memory verse to the team. They had a real opportunity to give, and they leapt at it.

When you get to experience what it's like to be the giver instead of the taker, it changes you. It changed Oscar, a fifth grader who lived in those slums. He joined us the day we were going door-to-door handing out bags of groceries.

His English was perfect. We asked Oscar about it, and he cried as he told us how he and his younger sister had been born in the United States. He'd attended school there. His father was there illegally, however, and when he was caught and deported, he brought his kids to the slum in Tijuana before heading back across the border to earn money for his family. Oscar was left to take care of his little sister.

"I know the only hope I have to get out of here is an education," he said, still crying as our team listened. I don't think there was a dry eye in hearing distance. His situation really brought humanity into the topic of immigration issues, revealing a gray area.

That was a turning point for me.

Because of meeting Oscar, I realized that simply being born on the other side of the border meant my life had been entirely different. I realized we've been blessed to be a blessing, not to simply soak it all in and expect more. God loves every kid, whether they're in the US, in Haiti, or in Mexico.

I didn't want my team to leave Tijuana feeling powerless, aware of something but not knowing what to do about it. So what were we supposed to do? Impossible situations mean you have to lean back and ask yourself what your gifting, skillset, and network are. You have to figure out how to leverage those in meaningful ways.

For me, the question that came to mind was, "Could I create an economy-resistant mechanism to provide consistent support?"

It was in that question that our One-to-One Program was born. For every student who pays tuition on a Valor campus, we use a portion of that tuition to sponsor a student's education in a developing nation. It's a unique global initiative which unites all Valor campuses around the world.

The problem with nonprofits is that too often, we walk around with our hand out instead of asking how to create a flywheel. We end up creating scarcity and a competitive dynamic in the community we're trying to help. Want to eat? Better get in line early. Want free clothing? Gotta be at the church. That approach isn't based in wisdom.

Wisdom Creates Paths, Not Positions

The starting point of wisdom is humility. Humility isn't some kind of awkward, fake humble-pride, but is instead made of a genuine desire to understand and to serve people.

Remember, the Bible tells us that wisdom is a fear of God, and fear of God is what humility is all about. We realize that there is a God, and I'm not him. That's humbling. It also drives us to ask questions to learn who God is and what he's all about. When we do that, we discover that he loves and serves humanity because he wants to save them, and he calls us to be imitators of him. It all comes full circle, back to the main point: loving and serving others.

Taking a fixed position keeps us from serving others.

When the Bible tells us to work out our own salvation (not anyone else's) with fear and trembling, it's telling us to guard ourselves from fixed mindsets and positions. We have to consistently challenge our thinking and assumptions, remembering that God's truth is *the* truth. There's a reason we lead people to Jesus instead of leading them to our own opinion and conclusions.

The opposite of a fixed position is wisdom in action, which is when there's kindness and mercy embodied in all that you do. Wisdom in action accepts someone as they are but, because of real love, won't leave them there. It'll tell you the truth. This is how wisdom creates paths; it makes people feel so loved and safe that they can work their journey out and get to Jesus. It knows we can't take someone else's journey for them, but that we can at least plant the seeds that have the potential for growth.

THE DIFFERENCE BETWEEN PATHS
AND PARKING LOTS

You can stay parked in one spot, believing what you've always believed, or you can take the journey from your current point of learning to God's throne room.

We do this at Valor in our learning, discipline, and behavioral processes on a global level. We help students make the paths, but what they do with those paths is up to them. These aren't confusing paths, mind you, but are intentional. They always point toward Jesus.

Not every Christian school creates paths. I've been to plenty of meetings with leaders of Christian schools in which the most concerning topics were questions about facial hair and nose rings. Those aren't path-creating concerns, and that's not a path-creating mentality. Their schools end up being parking lots, where kids are told what and how to believe with little room to question.

It's a mentality caught up in a culture war.

Culture is incredibly messy, and while we have to exist in culture, we aren't to conform to it. If all you see is a culture battle, all your paths lead to the battlefield. When leaders have an eye toward creating a life-giving path, the question is always whether or not something draws hearts back to Jesus.

Is this rule going to help bring kids to Jesus? Does this discipline create a path that will help kids find Jesus? If we change our policy, will it keep kids from getting to Jesus? Everything you confront starts with the question of whether or not the path leads to Jesus, because wisdom always wraps back around to find that answer.

Too often the questions we ask focus on specific behavior or sins, and we come out strong on one thing or another. If I won't accept an LGBTQ student but accept a student from a divorced family, what path did I create? What path did I block?

If we're going to set the captives free, you gotta get in the trenches with the captives. No one is judged into freedom. There's no need to be afraid of the trenches when you believe in absolute truth and know that true wisdom leads back to Jesus.

And frankly, regarding the LGBTQ question, we're going to lose even more kids because there's a massive number of Christian kids struggling with gender identity and sexual orientation right now. They're scared to even say anything because of where the conversation will leave them. They're afraid their parents will stop loving them if they even have the conversation.

"Love your kid," I told parents at a recent retreat. "We have kids struggling with this, and they need to be able to talk to you. You need to be able to frame it in a loving way so the path points to Jesus. You have to give them a safe space where they can seek God's truth about who he created them to be. Let the Holy Spirit do his work. It's our kindness that leads people to Jesus, where perfect love casts out fear."

God's not stupid. There's a reason why, in the first pages of the Bible, he tells us that he created people male or female. None of this culture shift we see today takes him by surprise, and it's worth noting that the Bible continues on from those first verses, all the way along a path that takes us straight to Jesus.

Calling out people's divine potential and destiny is for everyone, not just the people who look and live as I do. Maybe you didn't grow up in the trenches, but you ought to get down in them when the opportunity presents itself.

If you do that, you're one of the rare few. Since we tend to live in extremes, we see that secular private schools tend to be extremely liberal, while Christian private schools tend to be extremely conservative. I'm an equal opportunity offender, unwilling to lean either way, since the price of doing that is closing off a path to Jesus.

Our goal is to create pathways, regardless of your current position. Center-left, hard right, somewhere in the middle—it doesn't matter. There is always a path to Jesus from where you are, and that's what we want to help you find.

If you think this isn't feasible, consider what Jesus did. He intersected the lives of people from all walks of life. No matter who they were or what their political or personal beliefs were, he provided a path to himself. Not all took him up on the offer, but the path was there.

POSITIONING KIDS TO CHANGE THE WORLD

You can send a kid on a missions trip, or you can position them to change the world. It's not always the same thing. You can do more harm than good if you don't put a great amount of thought and collaboration into the process before shipping your kids off to the far reaches of the globe.

Our goal is to create pathways, regardless of your current position.

"You can change the world!" is the message that every possible media source drills into our kids' heads every day, but there's no positioning or preparation that makes such a thing possible. We set them up for failure because what could be worse than being aware of all that needs changing but having zero tools to make the change?

Yes, kids might stop using plastic drinking straws because they don't want them ending up in the ocean. There are good things they can do to help the environment. But there are many things pressed onto our kids in the name of "changing the world" that have minimal impact, at best leaving our children to be pawns in someone else's dreams and schemes. We end up with kids who are angry about the condition of the world with nothing to do but to find someone to blame.

Because of this, Valor positions our kids before they head out on a missions trip.

Long before the trip, we attach projects to it. For example, before a social studies class went to Mexico, they had to study immigration policies and problems. They got schooled on the position of both the left and the right. Then, when they got to Tijuana, the kids had to survey the people coming into the United States. This helped humanize what was motivating people to cross the border.

When they got back, they studied scripture. Using everything they'd learned and experienced, they were required to create a new immigration policy that acknowledged the real-world problems and challenges. Because yes, drug smugglers and criminals do take advantage of the porous border. How do we balance that with seeing the burdened and downtrodden in need of help? How do we create the path?

There were some great policy ideas that came from those kids because they weren't allowed to minimize humanity, nor did they have their head in the sand like some Pollyanna. It was entirely different than trying to grasp the issue by reading a textbook or listening to political leaders arguing back and forth.

The other option would be to send kids down there without getting them in a position to win. Without positioning, first-timers arrive on a missions trip and spend much of their time struggling to comprehend what they're experiencing. They don't have context or understanding for what they're seeing, and they certainly aren't positioned to make a lasting difference. People not positioned to win often end up making lousy decisions that neither identify nor solve actual problems. They can even make the situation worse.

When you position students to make real change, you can't take the position for them. No one can take a position for someone else; there's no cheating on the time and work it takes to come to understanding.

Christians are famous for jumping on the bandwagon without having much understanding of the wagon they're jumping on. The Common Core Standards Initiative is a great example. Basically, Common Core defines what elementary through high school students in the US should learn in core subjects at the conclusion of each grade, and students are tested and measured by those standards.

Christians love to hate Common Core, saying that it's dumbing down America. They grab data points to prove that kids who went through Common Core didn't do well on standardized tests, and that it functioned as some kind of ceiling that capped their potential.

I see Common Core as a floor, not a ceiling. It's a standard, not a curriculum. It's the starting point from which you build on. Common Core math is a popular target for hate, but what it does is try to show kids that there are a variety of ways to get the right answer. When people come to me and ask if we use Common Core at Valor, my question is simple. "Have you read all the standards? Which one is it that you don't like?"

I've never had a parent able to answer that question, yet some are making decisions about their child's school based on that alone. These are not thinking-based decisions, because they're not based in trying to understand first and conclude second. I'm not pro–Common Core at all, but my point is that we have to understand the problem before we can solve it.

Wisdom is a thinking position. It's an analyzing mode. It only comes through listening and understanding, two things we aren't encouraged to do in this sound-bite social media world.

Wisdom Doesn't Live in an Echo Chamber

If I was going to tell you what the pillars of wisdom looked like, I'd share something from my own journal, because it was a question I was asking myself:

1. Knowledge: everything starts with a basic level of knowledge based on an unchanging God in an ever-changing world.
2. Understanding: it's not simply enough to know God's word, but to understand it enough that you can act on it.
3. Discretion: you have to know when to speak and when to be quiet if you want to truly understand someone. We don't need big talkers, but instead, big doers.

4. Discernment: your intellect is defined by how well you discern. This is where faith is born.

5. Prudence: self-control will keep you from leading into the fear of man.

6. Humility: true humility comes from a deep reverence for, and fear of, God.

That's a beautiful list, but as strong as these pillars of wisdom are, they can't hold up in an echo chamber. The echo chamber is a massive beast in which wisdom cannot exist.

Remember the difference between creators and consumers? A creator mindset is curious and open, naturally asking questions while being discerning about the answers. They have to be discerning because they're always analyzing and using critical thinking as they make their way down the path. A creator is not afraid of asking controversial questions and seeking to understand another's viewpoint who may disagree with them. Because if there is an *absolute* truth, which I believe there is, we will only find it when we seek truth openly and honestly.

A creator is not afraid of asking controversial questions and seeking to understand another's viewpoint who may disagree with them.

Consumers are different. They are fixed in place and have a position mindset. They enjoy echo chambers, finding a great deal of comfort in familiarity and not having to think too hard about what they consume since it's all the same, anyway. A consumer hates to be challenged and hated on, and they love the status quo.

The best way to free a consumer from the echo chamber is through cognitive dissonance. When that contradictory information or experience flows across their brain, they may wake up.

Wisdom is about truth-seeking instead of trying to be right, and it has nothing to do with consuming. It's about winning people, not arguments.

THE 2020 PANDEMIC DESPERATELY NEEDED WISDOM

If ever we needed wisdom with its paths instead of its positions, it was during the pandemic.

Right or left, everyone was in a reactive mode, deciding where the battle lines were and taking a position before digging in. A different approach would be to lean into the Spirit of God. When you do that, he leads you down paths long before you realize you need to be on them.

Wisdom sees opportunities and can read the lay of the land. Two years before the pandemic, we launched Valor Global Online. We understand that God goes before us, and that he positions us for favor when we lean into him. In hindsight I can see God at work, though at the time it was painful; setting up the online school was a struggle all the way.

In December of 2017, while still in the midst of praying about what to do about the idea of an online school, I was on vacation in Cabo when I received a text from Doug Wood, a friend I hadn't spoken to in years. I found out they were in the hotel next to mine, and he asked if we could meet. The following day, I spent hours talking with Doug and Thea, and it was there that the dream of Valor Global Online took root.

We agreed to pray more, as it would be a significant investment for the Woods, and an online school would be a new adventure for me. I was still unsettled and not sure how to make it all work.

At a prophetic conference a few months later, I was praying that God would give me a clear direction on what to do. "God, should I do this? Should I partner with the Woods?" I prayed. "I don't need anything else but an answer to what to do."

A gentleman I didn't know came over and began to laugh as he was praying over me. "God's given you an entrepreneurial spirit!" he said. "That thing you've been praying about, wanting to know whether God's going to bless it? He says you should do it."

I forged ahead with the assurance that no man will thwart the plans God has for us.

Long before the hybrid model became common during the pandemic, we tried it at Valor. We'd invested heavily into tech and building the hybrid model, yet the consistent takeaway from each effort was that it was a substandard way to do education.

"No, this doesn't work," some of my best tech savvy teachers told me each time we tried to adjust what we were doing. "It's like having two different jobs. You have to teach online kids differently." The online teacher should only be teaching online, they said, while the classroom teacher should only teach in person. Otherwise, the experience for the online learner was awful, one where they ended up being mere viewers of the classroom instead of being engaged.

We readjusted, getting rid of the hybrid model and having pure online or pure classroom instruction.

By January 2020, we were exhausted. The online school wasn't getting the traction it needed, the cost to keep it running was high, and we were all tired. Then March 2020 rolled around, and the pandemic hit the United States.

Even while helping our brick-and-mortar schools navigate the changes happening, our online school grew quickly. Our staff can usually take July off, but we were onboarding so many new students in June, with a growing stack of applications, that we had to work straight through. I met with other Christian school principals, explaining how the pandemic was a chance for their schools to grow, if they took the opportunity.

Not only did this help our online school model thrive, but the influx of students meant we were able to better fund our One-to-One Program. By going online two years ahead of the game, we were positioned for a win.

Still, we learned from the pandemic. Most online schooling is content delivery, a kind of point-and-shoot curriculum. We continued to make changes to our online school because we understood that we instead had to focus heavily on each kid, making sure they're seen and heard each day. You can't call out their divine potential if you don't see or hear them.

As we checked in with our kids during the pandemic, we saw the negative effect it was having on them. They needed community and a reprieve from fearmongering. So we decided to flip the script and make our online school about community and focusing on the whole child. In January 2021, we had an in-person retreat in Arizona for those who wanted to attend, and from that, we came up with new ideas.

We require 100 percent camera-on attendance. We embed their FitBit data into their dashboard to make sure they're staying active, even providing advocates who help them set fitness goals. We have students do a self-check to see if they're feeling tired or unmotivated so they can identify a solution to the problem. We do this to teach them self-regulation and discipline embedded in daily habits. Otherwise we end up with cry rooms on secular college campuses.

A point-and-shoot information delivery system does nothing to tell kids that their emotions and feelings are real and valid and that there are things they can do to handle them.

Instead of online schooling being a lesser form of education where the student is isolated behind a screen with little expectation or accountability, we built it into a full education where the whole child was connected, was cared for, and mattered.

Wisdom is Leadership

Whenever you make wise decisions, you'll push up against conflict and criticism.

There's nothing I've done in starting Valor that hasn't gone uncriticized, whether it was the online school or the in-person retreat during a pandemic. This happens because wise decisions often don't go with the status quo. They aren't about preserving the comfort of the greatest common denominator, but are based on problem solving instead of symptom alleviation.

The only solution to this criticism is to lean into that tension. The obstacle in front of you is the way forward, and it's the way you get the strength to make it to the end. There's the old saying that flak is heaviest when you're over the target, and I'd go so far as to say that if you're not getting any flak, you're probably playing it too safe.

Another way to look at the leadership principles inherent in wisdom is to remember that wisdom creates paths, including those where none had previously existed. Wisdom dares to question the party line and hack a new path through the confusion to find a better way.

Wisdom is a big part of innovation, which is why true innovators get a solid dose of mockery before people realize they were right. Initially, wisdom might even look like foolishness, because we think common sense or practicality are the same as wisdom.

Having an in-person retreat in the midst of a restrictive pandemic was foolish, right?

The obstacle in front of you is the way forward, and it's the way you get the strength to make it to the end.

Except so much good came from it, not just with students, but with entire families. It was during that retreat that our families came up with family creeds that completely transformed them. It was during that retreat that we came up with methods to make online schooling more robust and more caring about the whole person. It was during the retreat that we created a community.

Common sense has never birthed true innovation or solved big problems. It's too far from the cutting edge to make a dent in anything. Of course, innovation isn't just about being edgy so you can justify poor ideas solely on their poor reception. True innovation is about pushing the envelope to find better solutions to big problems, something that ruffles feathers in a real way.

Wisdom can be counterintuitive because it starts with God. It's his sense, not human sense.

Common sense has never birthed true innovation or solved big problems.

We find wisdom in God's word, not humankind's words. The Bible is our roadmap for a whole and completely abundant life, and when you actually believe that, reading it is easier. Every time you open it up, you find gold. If you feel disconnected from your purpose in life, if you feel a bit lost, if you feel forgotten, it's through the Bible that you get back on the path wisdom has waiting for you. It's that understanding that we want to instill in kids at Valor.

LEADING OTHERS DOWN A NEW PATH

I was born and raised in South Dakota, and I didn't take a plane ride or see the ocean until I was in the tenth grade. I grew up in a white, conservative world. And while I'm very glad for the upbringing God gave me, it was during my first missions trip to Tijuana that cognitive dissonance slammed me in the gut, and I saw clearly for the first time.

I could see the border fence. I realized the importance of just a few feet on either side of the border making a world of difference. I didn't deserve to be born in the north, nor did I not deserve it; I just was.

Yet the same Spirit of God that fills me fills the people in the slums too.

One night while crying myself to sleep, I realized it was a privilege to have God break my heart for the same things that break his.

I'd walked through the world asleep, and while I gave lip service to the idea that God really loves the whole world, it had never really occurred to me until then. John 3:16 finally came alive for me, and I realized that my life had been filled with taking positions and having opinions, and that I had been letting my political views get ahead of my faith views. My conclusions weren't entirely based on God's truth, and they weren't based in true wisdom.

Wisdom creates paths, not positions. It sees the humanity in every person, helps us make an effort to understand one another, and pushes us out of our echo chambers so we can lead with an eye toward real change.

But I'm warning you: true wisdom can break your heart. And that's a good thing, because when you know that, you're ready to lead.

05

WHY GLOBAL MATTERS

Do a quick internet search on the landscape of the Philippines, and you'll see a green jeweled necklace spread out in the Pacific Ocean, a rolling mix of gently sloping earth punctuated by hills and mountains. Some of the mountains are volcanic, like Mount Mayon, which cuts into the sky southeast of Manila. Some of the mountains look like ancient giant moss-covered rocks, with rocky angles covered by what looks like a lush green carpet, making it tough to see where the mountains end and the hills and terraces begin.

But look past the tourist experience, and you'll find that some of the mountains are made of pure garbage.

When we think of the Smoky Mountains in the United States, we picture the beautiful hills of the southern Appalachians covered in old growth forest, with plant-generated fog wafting up from the valley floors. The Philippines had a Smoky Mountain too—a forty-year-old landfill heap in Tondo, Manila that emitted fumes and smoke from the toxic and frequently burning materials tucked inside. While this Smoky Mountain is now covered in plant growth that hides what lurks beneath, other sister trash mountains are growing.

Evangeline lived at the edge of one of these trash mountains, a giant mounded landfill that looked like a small mountain range with summits over a hundred feet tall. She was four years old, with a face like a little cherub, her shy smile evidence of a sweet spirit.

Like many countries, trash mountains are fringed by scavenger communities that spring up around the edges. These people make their living digging through the filthy trash, dodging sharp metal and broken glass, breathing in the smells of chemicals and putrefying food waste, all to find items to resell, recycle, or repurpose for income. This is where Evangeline called home.

We were there with our missions team for a week, doing what missions teams do. We played games with the kids, sang songs, and told Bible stories. We'd sit down and have lunch together, laughing and hugging. Evangeline sat next to me, and there, at the edge of the landfill, we had a little oasis of joy.

When lunch was over and our team was done for the day, I watched Evangeline pick up her lunch bag, break into her little smile, and then walk back toward the landfill, the towering profile of trash throwing a shadow across her small figure. I kept that picture in my head, zooming out and seeing young children bending over and picking up trash all around us.

Who's going to feed her tomorrow and the next day?

Either barefoot or in cheap flip flops that offered little protection from the dangers of a trash pile, they walked through the garbage, touching and considering the value of the things others had thrown out.

I fed her today, but what about tomorrow? I thought as I watched Evangeline disappear into the trash heap, her shirt blending into the mottled background of plastic trash bags and crumpled paper. *Who's going to help her read God's word?*

Who's going to feed her tomorrow and the next day?

This is the epitome of what's wrong with Christianity. It's easy to help someone once, and then leave them in their squalor. Every time I came home from a missions trip, I drowned in guilt and shame. My life was so extravagant compared to what I had just seen, compared to the people I had tried to help. I had a hard time praying for personal struggles because it seemed like I had no right to even come to God with a personal concern in comparison to what others around the world experienced. "This is hard, but at least I'm not living next to a mountain of trash," or "I'm really struggling right now, but how dare I complain because at least I know where my next meal is coming from."

This way of thinking traps you, leaving you unable to help others in the long-term, while also crippling your faith with guilt. But my experience with Evangeline, combined with a missions trip to India, brought some clarity on what I needed to do.

Seeing Evangeline experience a time of joy before heading back to the trash heap, or realizing that most of the church in India couldn't read and relied on one pastor and one Bible page for learning, distilled my dream: I wanted to help people everywhere learn how to read God's word.

The details of how that would actually look were a bit more complicated.

Is a School Possible Here?

Making your vision become reality is almost impossible if you're anchored to a plan B.

My current Christian school was devolving into an impossible situation (which we'll get into next chapter). While I knew I needed to leave to preserve my personal integrity, it was terrifying to think of going all in on my new dream. And I still didn't know exactly what that would look like. I had a couple of offers at competing schools, and it was tempting to get another safe job so I could keep gradually testing the water without leaping in.

God convicted me. I was reminded of how Abram was called to get up and leave the safety of everything he knew to go someplace God would direct him to. It was a place he was to head for without being sure of the actual destination. When God gives you a vision and a mission, there is no plan B. Plan Bs are distractions to keep you from succeeding.

I started having conversations with my friends Jeff Ahn and Sarah Byon, who lived in South Korea, about this idea I had for a school. He'd been with me on the trip to the Philippines, and he'd seen the same things I had. How would we go about getting someone like Evangeline in a school with a Christian education so she could grow in God's word?

Jeff knew of Jeong Rye, a Korean missionary doing work near the landfill and meeting weekly with children. He asked her, "Would a school be possible here?" We listened closely to what she had to say based on her own experiences. While it was possible, it was improbable—but I believe improbable is great odds when both God and a committed group of people are involved.

We dreamed about this idea for a school in the US that could help little girls like Evangeline. We created a Valor development team and dreamed along the lines of: if we could do anything we wanted and produce the caliber of students we wanted, what would that look like?

First and foremost, this school would fund other kids. This is the One-to-One Program we eventually came up with, where the tuition for a Valor student also covered the tuition for a student overseas. Jeff and I had already started a business where we placed foreign exchange students in schools and had been using that money as seed money to pay for other kids' tuitions. That idea was already in motion for me, and it was something I wanted to continue.

More than anything, I wanted this school to reflect the heart of Jesus, even more than I wanted it to be about the change it could bring in our kids. When I read the scriptures, I had to ask myself if we were giving our kids the opportunity to not just memorize God's word, but actually practice it. We expect our kids to grow up and be missional-minded and generous, but do we ever have them practice that? Anyone who has played a musical instrument, excelled at sports, or nurtured a natural talent knows that how you practice is how you play.

What are our kids practicing? Self-focus? Self-centeredness? Or are they practicing generosity with a global perspective? I've always found it fascinating the number of parents and educators who are so incongruent on this. John Donne told us that no one was an island and that we are all interconnected, and while we might nod our heads in agreement, we still raise our kids as islands.

My dream wasn't just about helping kids like Evangeline. It was also about honoring and practicing biblical mandates instead of being all talk without much walk. There are over two hundred Bible verses about taking care of the poor and the widowed. How could I walk it out myself and teach kids to do the same?

James 1:27 quickly became a catalyst for me. "Religion that God our Father accepts as pure and faultless is this: to look after orphans and widows in their distress and to keep oneself from being polluted by the world." I wanted to use that to ignite a similar fire in the lives of my students. I wanted to help the Evangelines of the world by encouraging the kids in our school to live that out themselves. Could you imagine what the world would look like if every Christian school took on this mission? We'd quickly close the education gap and spread the Gospel at the same time.

We expect our kids to grow up and be missional-minded and generous, but do we ever have them practice that?

The Hidden Scaffolding in Our Lives

An interesting by-product of this focus is that you find what your life has been built on. We all have constructs from our upbringing, and we aren't usually aware of how they dictate what we think or how we respond to what's happening around us. When you help kids grasp a global understanding of the world, it's not just the global community and culture you're exposing them to. You also expose them to themselves. They get a look at that underlying structure for the first time, seeing how it does (and doesn't) work with the larger reality of the world around them.

I fully realized this when I was with a group of high school girls in Tijuana, Mexico on a missions trip. On our way back, we walked across the border instead of driving. On the American side of the border there was a restroom. This was very much an American-built structure, noticeably different from what we'd experienced during a week in the slums of Tijuana. We walked in, and the girls ran over to the sink, giggling and smiling. They flipped on the water, washing their hands and splashing a bit on their faces.

"I've never been so grateful for running water," one said as the other nodded, shoving her hands back under the cold water gushing from the faucet.

That was the first time it really hit me that there are so many things in everyday life that I didn't even realize were a privilege. When my children asked me for a drink of water in the middle of the night, I went to the sink and got them a clean glass of water. A UNICEF report shows that, for a third of the world, that's not how it works.[12] You'd have to walk a ways to get your water, and it probably wouldn't be clean.

Exposing our kids to things that forced them to confront their assumptions became intentional. They couldn't assume clean running water was always going to be available. They couldn't assume that the people they were trying to share Jesus with could read. To help my kids (and so many others) not only understand this, but do something about it, I again looked abroad, this time to a small village in India.

A Christian couple went to a village to begin a school—they were the only Christians in the village. They announced that they would make the school available to anyone, including the untouchables, which shocked everyone.

The caste system in India is a hierarchy of hereditary social groups based on their occupation. At the top are the Brahmins (usually the ones to be educated), followed by the Kshatriyas, the Vaishyas, and the Sudras. But there's a basement level of that pyramid, a group previously known as the untouchables, or Dalits. They're allowed to clean things, but that's about it. This last group is often shunned and excluded. For them to be included in the offer of an education was unthinkable.

These Christians started by teaching stories out of the Bible, but they changed the names as they told the stories. No one knew they were teaching the kids the Bible as a path to reading for the first three years. Not even the Hindu teachers at the school realized what they were teaching. The village quickly grew to trust

[12]"1 In 3 People GLOBALLY Do Not Have Access to Safe Drinking Water – Unicef, Who," World Health Organization (World Health Organization, June 18, 2019), https://www.who.int/news/item/18-06-2019-1-in-3-people-globally-do-not-have-access-to-safe-drinking-water-unicef-who.

them because of how they loved their kids and the good education they gave.

Gradually they used the real names of the people from the Bible. Then they begin introducing prayer. And this is where the transcendent transformation began.

We had an opportunity to be with these principals and listen to their story. One of the boys who came to their school, a Dalit street cleaner, became a Christian, eventually growing up to become the mayor of the village. The transformational power of the Gospel made the impossible happen.

But it wasn't only the adults on the missions team who heard about how they put everything on the line. Our kids were there too, staying in a compound where young Muslims who converted to Christianity lived. Our kids met eighteen- and nineteen-year-olds who faced rejection, beatings, and possibly death because they converted to Christianity and would be pastors. The persecution was real and severe. This was a new reality, one in which our kids saw people their age completely relying on the power of prayer.

> **Just like I saw with the running water near the Mexican border, I watched kids wake up to reality and to true gratitude.**

Just like I saw with the running water near the Mexican border, I watched kids wake up to reality and to true gratitude. Kids who suffered from anxiety shed those chains as they stopped focusing on the self and looked outward. It was amazing to watch the transformational power of the Gospel happen to both groups, the people in India and the people on our team. Months after the trip, I'd have parents come up to me and tell me how much their kids had changed. "They don't complain at home. They don't complain about doing chores," they'd tell me. "They're so different now."

The change was catching. Scared, sheltered-in-place students were all vying for the most dangerous overseas missions trips they could get on, going from wanting to be safe and comfortable to wanting to change the world.

Moving From Apathy to Impact

It was clear that if we were going to start a school, the global piece had to be in place.

We could see the effect it had on the kids who went on these overseas trips. It was something we wanted built into the school itself so that apathy about the world around them wasn't allowed to grow in our students' hearts. But how do we do that? How could we move our affluent students from apathy to impact?

Our kids walk through life constantly comparing themselves to each other, which leads to complaining instead of any real action. They gripe that they don't get the latest cellphone, or that they don't get enough followers on social media. In many of our public schools, they've been taught to hate America rather than acknowledge the nation's imperfections while still being grateful for the opportunities available to those born here. They have cushy lives they come to both require and loathe, and we're frustrated that all they could grow out of that easy ground was complaints. Yet what kind of opportunities do we provide kids to see things differently and to become aware of what they have?

We do it through a global approach that shifts the culture. Once someone gets a global perspective, they can step back and appreciate what they have. And more importantly, they can then understand that they have a responsibility to add their value into the world. Once you experience the true chaos of extreme poverty, it's easier to see the goodness in your own life and how to make use of it.

We also make sure parents understand they are a part of this. Right out of the starting gate, they have to be givers. If parents aren't willing to get out of their comfort zone, their kids certainly wouldn't be. The school we were creating wouldn't be a good fit at all. This applies to our staff too. They have to be willing to travel internationally with high school students to hard places. If that's off the table, they're probably not a great fit for the school either.

By setting up this foundation, we built a system that drew world-changing culture to our doorstep. We had to, because there was no way I could create a school with a business-as-usual mindset, churning out book-smart students completely self-absorbed and disconnected from the world in, where more than half of its citizens live on less than $2 each day. Or where more than two hundred million kids have zero access to education. There are endless stats like this, painting a mind-numbing picture of need and disparity. There was no way we could create a school without building into it a heart for serving and for missions work.

That heart, in a person and in an institution like a Christian school, is at the core of serving Christ. No one is exempt from this call.

Jeff and I had created the ministry using money from placing students to send other kids to school, and we needed to move it from the side and place it front and center. It was too important to exist in the margins, too central to what it meant to be a disciple of Christ.

So that was the key: global missions had to be the heart of the school. But lasting impact meant consistency, so instead of a shotgun approach where we showed up and dumped a load

There was no way we could create a school without building into it a heart for serving and for missions work.

of toys and clothing at an orphanage only to be followed up by another missions team doing the same thing after we left, we wanted to be changemakers. It's not enough that we left with a warm, fuzzy feeling because we did something "good" for an orphanage. We didn't make any real positive change. You can't just put your week in, check off the box, take the selfie, and move on. We needed to leave a lasting impact in every life involved in the process, whether it was someone like Evangeline or the students themselves.

Staff, students, and their entire families would be put on this mission. If you chose to send your kids to our school, you were accepting that you were going to be asked to constantly level up and that there would never be a comfort zone you could rest in. A few people engaging once in a while with the Great Commission when it suits them doesn't work. We're *all* in, and we're all-in.

06

HOW OUR KIDS CHANGE
THE WORLD

Back from the Philippines with the weight of what I'd seen and this vague idea of starting a new school, I returned to my job at the Christian school. The situation there hadn't improved, and the gnawing sense of creating a school with the potential for global impact while working in what seemed an impossible situation created an internal clash that was unbearable.

I'd received a scholarship to go to an innovation in education conference in Davos, Switzerland, and the timing couldn't have been better. Getting away on a trip I could not have afforded on my own at the time, with a chance to mix with hundreds of top educators from around the world, was exactly what I needed. The keynote speaker was Sir Ken Robinson, a British expert on education, and while the conference itself was not a Christian event, it soon became clear that God had his hand on everything that transpired.

For one of our evening conference meals, we were to go to the top of a nearby mountain. I hopped on a gondola to take me up to the location and found myself crammed into a fully packed car, squeezed next to a man I'd never before seen in my life. We began talking about education issues.

"What makes your heart bleed?" the man finally asked me.

That's when I started telling him about Evangeline, the little girl who lived at the landfill in the Philippines, and how I was trying to figure out how to start schools in places like that while also helping affluent students be a part of the equation. The more I talked, the more the words flowed together. It was the first time I remember actually giving voice to what Valor would become, finding the words to organize the jumble of thoughts in my head. It's internally galvanizing when you can put structure to an ambiguous idea.

As the gondola slid into the station at the top of the mountain and everyone positioned themselves to exit, the man reached into his jacket pocket and pulled out his business card.

"I'd like you to participate in Harvard's think tank on global education in the spring," he said, handing me the card. It turns out that I was talking to the dean of Global Education from Harvard all this time, unaware. "Look me up, and when you apply, mention this meeting on your application."

I either had to let go of my vision or truly grab hold of it.

Despite that great mountaintop experience, I had to go home sometime. And when I did, I found the same situation waiting for me at the school I was working at. Maybe it was going to the mountaintop and having fresh vision that made the job more difficult, but it seemed as if things deteriorated more quickly than before. The Harvard think tank opportunity was forgotten as I tried to figure out what to do at work. By January, months later, I knew I couldn't keep my job and hold onto my integrity. I either had to let go of my vision or truly grab hold of it.

In February my business partner Jeff called me from South Korea. Our plans to take the leap and start Valor had heated up, but he'd heard about something he thought I'd be interested in.

"I was just talking to a friend about a global education think tank at Harvard," he said. "She thinks she could help us get in."

The man on the gondola! I thought, remembering the business card. "Hold on," I said. "I have the business card from the man who's running it."

The think tank was limited to fifty educators from around the world, and the fact that both Jeff and I got in was nothing short of a miracle. For Jeff, the Ivy League was nothing new. He'd attended those schools and fit right in. But for me, the crazy dreamer from a small Christian school who grew up in South Dakota? The only reason I got in was because of the crowded gondola ride on the way up the mountain and the conversation I'd had where I finally gave voice to my dream.

The Global Perspective Works from Every Angle

It's one thing to have an idea that you think is solid, something you've experienced yourself and believe would work on a larger scale, but it's much better to have broad data to back it up. Jeff and I traveled to the Harvard campus that May, and while I could talk about the think tank experience for hours, the most amazing piece for us was how our vision for a different kind of school was echoed in the research we received.

The data showed that our American system of education was broken, which wasn't a surprise to us. But the data went on to show that in order to prepare our kids well for the future, we had to take a global perspective. The future was global, and it was screaming full speed toward our kids, whether they were ready for it or not.

Even though this was all from a secular perspective, I'd arrived with a biblical worldview that had already told me God's heart was for the whole world and that our kids needed to grasp that. Here I had research that backed up and validated what God was speaking to me, and I was beyond convinced of the vision of the school we were meant to set up. I felt that global perspective mattered, and now I really knew it.

But that wasn't all. In my mind, I could see Evangeline as she was when I first met her, and I could imagine her as she might be if we were to start a school that would change her future. But I was taking a guess at how things might go. Was this truly viable?

In answer to my unspoken question, that man I'd spent so much time talking to on the gondola stood up and spoke to all of us assembled there for the think tank. He shared his personal story of being a small boy in an impoverished village in Venezuela. Christian nuns had started a school there and made sure he received an education. And now here he was, the dean of Global Education at Harvard University. There were great possibilities for Evangeline.

Connecting Global Families, One-to-One

"Angie," God was telling me. "It's time to let go."

After years of fighting policies, boards, entrenched ideas, and myself, to the point where I'd begun to experience it in my physical body, I was at a crossroads. I'd gone from the public education system to the Christian school movement and was questioning whether I should leave education altogether or start my own school.

"We've had principals before you, and we will have principals after you. You don't actually understand business like you think you do," I was told at my job. It was an idea that went entirely against my belief of every person being uniquely gifted and placed by God.

Even though God had been putting the pieces into place to start a school, I was still holding onto job security and struggling to give up what I'd worked so hard to build. This was the school that had helped me go to India for the first time, a trip that had completely changed me. There was a confusing mix of emotions about how to compartmentalize it all. Even considering switching jobs didn't bring peace; tentatively interviewing to be a principal at other schools led to the discovery that their vision was already in place, and it wasn't the vision God had given me.

"Angie, even Jesus needed Pontius Pilate to deliver the savior of the world," my husband told me one evening after I voiced my struggle with work. It was a profound statement that helped me see the value of the difficult situation I was in. New wine from crushed grapes, gold refined in fire, the malleable clay on the potter's wheel, Joseph's audacious dreams that landed him in prison before he made his way to the palace. Me giving up my job as principal of a Christian school and walking in faith toward the vision God had given me.

God had been preparing me my whole life. Everything had a purpose, and I wasn't going it alone. My mother took frequent 911 calls from me, listening to what was happening in my life and interceding in prayer. My dear friend Rashell Linenberger not only worked with me but helped keep me anchored in truth. These two encouraging prayer warriors gave me the courage to take bold steps.

In one year I went from a trash mountain in the Philippines to a mountain gondola in Switzerland to participating in a global education think tank . . . to walking away from my job and starting a school. When God moves, he does it beyond our control, and he doesn't waste time.

Jeff, Sarah, and I—the Valor development team—didn't waste time either, though we were figuring things out as we went.

In March we had the initial meeting I wrote about in chapter two. Parents signed up and paid an enrollment fee of $100, even though we didn't know how much we should charge for tuition yet. We didn't have nonprofit status or even a bank account set up. Soon it was May, and we weren't even sure where the physical location of our school would be. We told the families that we'd know if the school was going to happen by June 1. If I didn't have a school building by that date, we were going to have to postpone the launch. The crazy thing was that, despite these obstacles, Valor was growing. My personal cell phone was blowing up from parents ready to enroll their kids and put down money.

What we were sure of was the idea of one-to-one, where the tuition for a student in the US school we were starting would help fund a school overseas. We'd already made a commitment to start a kindergarten school in the Philippines. We decided that even if our US Valor school didn't get off the ground, we'd simply plan to fundraise to meet that commitment.

I was preparing to send out a letter on June 2, telling our families that we'd have to postpone opening the school for a year. But then, at 10 p.m. on June 1, Pastor Jess Strickland of Living Hope Church generously gave us a location on their church campus. We wouldn't have to pay rent until October.

Just four days later, on June 5, we started our Valor Philippines school campus, and suddenly we understood how much tuition would be to cover a student there as well as one here. I can't begin to describe how messy the numbers were at first as we worked our way through starting the school. More than once, the cart definitely came before the horse.

Still, we gained credibility and favor. God's hand was definitely in this work, and people from the school I had left as principal wanted to be a part of what we were doing without me even asking. Some began helping us with public relations and marketing.

As our school in the US grew, we realized we didn't have enough kids in our Philippines school because we'd committed to having one global student for every student in the US. Since the kids in the village hadn't been to school, we'd started with only kindergarten. You can't put a kid in third grade if they've never been to school before.

We were committed to the One-to-One Program, though, and decided we needed to find more kids for the overseas school option. A friend of mine, Joey Jenkins, had been working with orphans in Haiti. We connected with him, and pretty soon we'd partnered with an orphanage in Haiti to send their kids to an established Christian school. Now we had school connections in both Haiti and the Philippines. We even took students and the school board over to watch our first kindergarten graduation in the Philippines.

As amazing as it was, we quickly discovered a problem.

When Global Problems Become Local Curriculum

Starting the school in the Philippines and building partnerships in Haiti was a beginning, but there was more we needed to do. We couldn't just throw money at the problem. Kids were coming to school sick from dirty water. Teachers needed more training.

"How can we bring our American students into the equation and make them part of the solution?" we wondered, which is how the problems our global schools were facing became part of our local curriculum.

This is when we learned the importance of asking questions of those you serve rather than assuming you know the best solution. It's where the idea that wisdom creates paths was born and when we realized the power of long-term obedience in the same direction rather than one-off missions trips.

The impact this had in our overseas schools was easy enough to spot. You can see the benefits of clean water pretty quickly. But we saw a real impact on our own kids when they had these global experiences. For example, our kids come home with a profound sense of gratitude for our Constitution and for our infrastructure. When you get a real taste of what life is without those things, you appreciate them more.

Unfortunately, research shows us that 11 percent of Americans have never even left the country—much less students.[13] One hundred percent of Valor kids will have gone overseas, most to multiple countries. I'd wager that a lot of young people who dislike America are likely untraveled or, if they have traveled, have never ventured beyond the Western tourist experience. Too many in America are getting their understanding of the global community from the TV or social media, an approach that desensitizes and skews understanding rather than leading to it. We end up with a mushy "globalism" where the richness and uniqueness of different cultures are blurred or erased, with kids standing under the banner of celebrating differences when they are actually poorly equipped to know how to identify and value differences at all.

---

[13]Lea Lane, "Percentage of Americans Who Never Traveled beyond the State Where They Were BORN? A Surprise," Forbes (Forbes Magazine, June 29, 2021), https://www.forbes.com/sites/lealane/2019/05/02/percentage-of-americans-who-never-traveled-beyond-the-state-where-they-were-born-a-surprise/?sh=7ba95c172898.

If we don't build a global perspective into our curriculum, it doesn't happen.

It's too much money to travel overseas. We're too tired to make it happen. Kids are busy with music lessons and other activities. But then pretty soon they've grown up, and we've missed the opportunity because no day was the day we took global action.

If we rely on a traditional approach to teaching students about the world around them, they understand concepts instead of cultures. They can recite facts but don't know how to take action. The fruit of understanding is action and an opportunity to develop habits in their life that lead to positive change. Getting an A on a test does none of that. It doesn't even signify comprehension. If you give a kid the same test a year later, do they remember anything?

Global Works, No Matter the Worldview

A global perspective to the local curriculum has merit, whether you look at it from a secular worldview or a Christian one.

From a secular standpoint, our kids are able to cross cultural boundaries, engage in meaningful conversations, and collaborate with people all around the world. They have an enlarged perspective and are able to interpret and understand the context of what's going on in the world much better than someone who's never left their home state. A global perspective is good for your business and future, particularly for those who are creators. Being exposed to different cultures gives you a richer repository to draw from when it comes time to problem solve and create something new. You've seen, heard, and tasted things outside your comfort zone. You have more to reference.

The fruit of understanding is action and an opportunity to develop habits in their life that lead to positive change.

It also exposes the many areas the United States has to grow and improve. In fact, one of our goals has been to fuse some of the most beautiful elements of our global community into our own culture. For example, our Korean friends have a beautiful tradition of honoring elders in their culture. The way they show respect for aging people in their community is something I admire deeply. There is so much wisdom to be found there. And that is just one example of how exposure to global culture and values can lend itself to improving our own.

From a Christian standpoint, a global perspective is a small picture of what is happening (and will happen) in heaven. The Bible tells us that there are people of every tribe, nation, and tongue. The church is made up of people across time and culture, and a global education touches on all that. It is absolutely biblical that we love and care about the poor and the needy wherever they are and that we view people in other countries as our brothers and sisters.

A global perspective is one that acknowledges that God loves the whole world. It instills empathy for others and gratitude for what you have. It creates much-needed cognitive dissonance. It wakes up our subconscious lives that want to function in a default mode, a mode that allows us to wander through life half-asleep and lets others make decisions for us by our nonaction.

Being exposed to different cultures gives you a richer repository to draw from when it comes time to problem solve and create something new.

Current education systems feed that default state of existence on an epic level by forcing kids into consistent routines that require habit instead of thought. "Do x, y, and z, and then take a quiz," the system says, instead of throwing the unexpected at them and forcing them to sit up and think.

One of the questions I get asked is why our One-to-One Program doesn't partner with schools in the US. My response is that, in this country, if you want a way out, you can find one. You can get an education, you can get food, you can grab at an opportunity and use that to boost yourself into a position to grab at a rung higher up. In any place in this country, this is 100 percent true, no matter who tries to tell you otherwise.

It is not true for every other country. I've met people who watched their children starve to death because there was no help, no safety net, no other resource. They were on their own, and their children starved. My calling, and the vision for Valor, is to show up in those countries where no one else is.

I consider myself an American patriot, but we get into trouble when we forget that God loves the whole world. He doesn't love us more than he loves others, and he wants to love them through us. I think of the many missions trips I've been on where I'm in a worship service, and I don't understand the language, and maybe the music is a bit too loud, and the sounds and smells are very unlike my home church . . . and yet the Spirit of God is there. It's the same Spirit I've encountered all around the world, among God's people.

If you long to be faithful to God's word and his command to go into the world and love one another, you have to think globally.

07

WE DON'T WHINE!

Kambiri, Kenya is found in the western part of the
African nation, near the border of Uganda. It sits
northeast of massive Lake Victoria, at the edge of
Kakamega National Reserve.

Whenever we take a missions trip to visit our
school there, our American kids become teachers of
sorts. There are games and educational activities,
and our kids teach a class or lead in devotionals.

At the end of the day, we dance. It's a standard
practice in Kenya to close out the day with a traditional dance, and so the Kenyan kids and the staff
teach our kids the dance. Everyone joins together,
and never have you seen American kids as curious
and engaged, laughing and talking, as you do in that
moment.

There's a natural ebb and flow of who is teacher
and who is student. One minute our kids are leading a class, the next they are being taught to dance.
It's an incredibly valuable exchange of culture.

But there's a fence.

In that beautiful celebration of the end of the
day, with its laughing and talking, where our three
hundred Kenyan students are clean and fed and
wearing crisp uniforms, there are kids outside
the fence. Their clothes show wear and fit poorly.
Most don't have any shoes on their feet. They are
dirty and hungry. They literally press their faces up
against the fence around the school property, fingers gripping the wire, watching us sing and dance.

merican student came up to me and motioned
hed up at the fence. "Do you see those kids on
other side of the fence?" she asked.

I nodded.

"We have to figure out how to get them on this side of the
fence," she said.

Americans get a bad rap when it comes to travel, and it's
because we often act in stereotypical ways. We can be loud, and
since we come from a very individualistic culture, we aren't very
inclusive. We aren't always aware of the impact we have on the
people around us and come off as rude.

But this girl saw beyond the boundaries.

It was a powerful moment for one of our kids to see that there
is more work to be done, even in the busyness and activity of
the moment. Even better, she took action. She didn't ask me to
do something, but wanted to be part of the solution and to take
ownership.

Each missions trip has enlarged our perspective and
informed what we do in the classroom. We watch our kids both
teach and learn within a different culture. This teaches us how to
teach them, meaning the world really has become our classroom.

What that girl did was take the time to see a problem and follow through with a solution. She put it into practice.

Having a Solutions-Oriented Mindset

Typically, problems are something we complain about rather
than solve, because complaining is easier. We live in a world
that sees problems everywhere, but most people rarely get past
complaining.

One thing we do at Valor is incorporate the process of thinking there is always an answer to a problem. Always. You have to believe that first. Let's use my own kids at home as an example.

"I'm hungry," my kids might say to me.

"Rephrase that," I'll say.

It's easy enough to state a need, but we do it in a way that puts the burden on someone else to solve. My own kids have been trained to state things differently. Instead of "I'm hungry," they'll ask, "May I have something to eat?"

That's entirely different because it's thinking in terms of a solution.

They still recognize the need, but they are verbalizing it with a solution packaged in the request. It's about training them to solve a problem rather than whine about it, and while it might seem strange that I do this, even those little statements in moments matter. These patterns of thinking become habits that stick with them to adulthood.

We take this approach with the parents of our students. We never want them to be at home, frustrated, thinking of all the things they wish the teachers would do differently. Instead, we want them to come and sit at the table with us so we can talk it out. A solutions-oriented mindset always has an eye for what isn't working partnered with an ability to think about what would make it work.

The belief that there is always a solution to a problem is key, but what we find is that most people are more comfortable and content to live in the status quo that says "this is a broken system, and we can't do anything about it but complain."

Nearly all the Ivy League schools tell us the educational system is broken. Research agrees. Leading innovative companies

One thing we do at Valor is incorporate the process of thinking there is always an answer to a problem. Always.

chime in and say the same thing, informing us that they don't like hiring students out of college because they're not prepared for the world. Everyone is saying that it's terrible, that it's broken . . . but they don't offer a real solution.

Again, complaining is easy. Taking personal responsibility to insert yourself into the equation and offer up a solution in these broken spaces is hard.

Isn't that what Jesus does?

He's the ultimate bridge builder, finding what's broken and not leaving it that way. He quenched true spiritual thirst with living water, and he talked to the outcasts. He showed himself to be the one man who wouldn't take advantage of people's problems. He healed the sick who'd been that way for so long that the people who saw them begging had come to see their brokenness as the way it would always be.

The Christ-centered model doesn't walk past what's broken. It says that there are solutions, and that we are part of them. If we're going to wake up our kids to this reality, we can't let them complain. We have to push back against their whining and teach them to reframe every situation.

A solutions-oriented mindset always has an eye for what isn't working partnered with an ability to think about what would make it work.

You're thirsty? What are you going to do about it?

You got an F? What are you going to do to turn it into a win?

We live in a broken world full of problems, yes, but between the Heavenly Father's gifts and creativity and our society's technology, anything is possible. If you don't understand this, you look away from problems instead of at them. If you have an abundant solutions-oriented mindset, problems don't scare you because you live in a limitless world where problems are solvable instead of insurmountable. Positioning our kids with that idea will change the world.

All this starts by recognizing the blessing of God in our lives and having a heart that is always thankful for the resources he entrusts to us to use for good. Being unable to see how God has blessed us makes it difficult to see his abundance and makes it almost impossible to have a solutions-oriented mindset.

Don't think God has blessed you? Taken care of you? Then your eyes are on your problems, and there's no solution that's greater.

Status Quo Mindset	Solutions-Oriented Mindset
I'm bad at math.	If I get a tutor, I can understand.
My job is boring.	I could pursue promotion, job development training, or look for a new career.
My boss doesn't understand me.	By careful observation, I can figure out how my boss best communicates.
The coach won't play me during games.	If I practice more and talk to the coach about areas of improvement, I might be able to play.

Without a solutions-oriented mindset, you're stuck in the status quo, complaining and never moving past whatever it is that's taking the joy out of your life. You'll be an angry, helpless victim, controlled by circumstances.

Reality is a Matter of Focus

Imagine you're at a car lot, and you decide to buy a Ford Fusion.

You've never seen this kind of car before, and you think it's amazing. You love your new car and are so excited to drive it and catch the attention of everyone else. Except once you own the car, you start to see Ford Fusions everywhere. At the grocery store, at church, driving down the street—it feels like everyone has a Ford Fusion!

This same thing happened to me when I was pregnant. Before that, I never really noticed pregnant women. But once I was pregnant, suddenly I noticed that tons of women were pregnant; it seemed like they were everywhere.

Once our brain learns something, we're triggered to recognize it. This is because our brain stem has a network of neurons called the reticulating activating system (RAS). This system has several functions, but one of them is to help us put context to what our senses are experiencing. It connects the subconscious part of our brain with the conscious.

We can tell them that needs exist, but until they experience it, they never really notice.

Until you own the car, you don't realize how many others do too. Until I was pregnant, I didn't notice pregnant women. Once our brains have the sensory experience, we make those connections. It expands our vision.

Think of the girl who saw those kids on the other side of the fence. In all the noise and activity of the dancing students, she saw beyond the fence. Why was she able to do that?

We are training our students to look for needs, and part of the way we do it is through experience. We can tell them that needs exist, but until they experience it, they never really notice. That's when they realize they have gifts and talents to offer, because seeing need helps them recognize how they can uniquely answer it. They go from having to learn how to look for opportunities to realizing them. It's the difference between looking for a table and realizing that God is setting the table for them.

We'll miss that God-loaded table if we're walking through life asleep, if we live in a conforming system where we can get As without thinking. The routines that kids (and their parents) fill their day with to get the grades or the paycheck unfortunately allow them to function on autopilot.

One of the habits we've established in our online school is morning check-in, where we ask our students to tell us five things they're grateful for.

Gratitude is the key to disengaging that autopilot. Research shows that people who express gratitude are able to look at the future with more hope.[14] They are more resilient, no matter what life throws at them. Practicing gratitude (which indicates it doesn't just happen on its own) reduces the negativity that festers in your mind and your words, spreading negativity to others.[15] Because you're not focusing on yourself so much, you're less depressed and down. It's like a chain reaction to better mental and, consequently, physical health.

Of course, we don't let our students tell us the same five things every day either. They have to really think about it. Our kids are now on the lookout for things to be grateful for and are too busy focusing on gratefulness to live a life of comparison.

Ralph Waldo Emerson got it right when he said, "Sow a thought and you reap an action; sow an act and you reap a habit; sow a habit and you reap a character; sow a character and you reap a destiny."

---

[14]Christopher Bergland, "An Attitude of Gratitude: Why Saying 'I Am Grateful' Matters," *Psychology Today* (Sussex Publishers, January 23, 2021), https://www.psychologytoday.com/us/blog/the-athletes-way/202101/attitude-gratitude-why-saying-i-am-grateful-matters.

[15]"Gratitude," *Psychology Today* (Sussex Publishers), accessed September 28, 2021, https://www.psychologytoday.com/us/basics/gratitude.

Something as simple as learning to find what they're grateful for makes them aware of opportunity, which helps them see what God is laying out before them, which gears them for finding solutions to problems, which is how they change the world.

What's hard for adults to understand is you can't just say this to them. One of our common principles at Valor is that just because we teach it doesn't make it so, not until we've seen it practiced.

You can't say things to kids and expect it to take, as noble and correct as those words might be. You can talk all about the qualities of the Ford Focus, but they'll never really notice until they go for a ride or watch you drive it.

Unfortunately, today's education system is more focused on content. We're busy jamming information into kids, quizzing them on the car manual and diagrams of the engine instead of giving them time and space to drive it.

If we slow the rollout of content and give them more opportunities to think about and practice solving problems, kids will have an activated RAS. They're naturally inclined to take note of what's going on around them instead of being oblivious or seeing problems and whining about them.

When you see kids unable to see or solve problems, you have to ask where they were trained. It was done over time with parents who didn't pay attention to what their kids were watching and practicing. It was a slow burn of teachers talking through a lesson and chugging through a curriculum, thinking we were preparing them for the world, only to see them explode in anger and light cities on fire and spray graffiti everywhere.

It's what the kids actually *do* that prepares them for the world, not what we say.

"Education is the answer!" is not a true statement, because it matters what kind of education you're giving kids. Parents and

It's what the kids actually *do* that prepares them for the world, not what we say.

teachers' behaviors, and the permissiveness of victimized behavior whether intentional or not, is part of education.

Going Beyond Maslow

A monkey and a fish went to school. In the middle of the playground was a tall tree.

"Whoever climbs the tree first is the smartest!" the teacher said, pulling out her stopwatch.

While the monkey clapped before racing toward the tree, the fish flopped on the ground. Master of the pond, he was a failure with the tree.

This is how our education system works.

We measure kids and teachers based on how well they can regurgitate facts based on a curriculum, itself based on standards. To justify expenditure and policy, we have to have measurements. To have measurements, we have to have standards. This has been the reality (and problem) no matter what political party is in office.

You cannot possibly lay out the same requirements for all kids and expect an equal outcome. There's no way using standards like we do measures anything of value. We hand kids the same things as if they're all the same, not taking into account that their Creator designed them for a different destiny.

"Climb the tree, no matter how you were designed!" we say, and then wonder why kids fail.

In 1943, Abraham Maslow introduced the hierarchy of needs. His theory was that the most basic of human needs must be met first, with following levels building on those met needs. The three groupings are basic needs, followed by psychological needs, and capped off with self-fulfillment needs. In order, from the bottom to the top, the needs are as follows:

- Basic needs: physical needs like food, water, rest, and warmth, followed by security and safety.
- Psychological needs: feelings of belonging and being loved, which can then be followed by a sense of accomplishment.
- Self-fulfillment needs: reaching our full potential, exercising our creativity.[16]

Maslow stops at needs being met, not what your destiny is, so we took this a step further at Valor by trying to make sure we understand who you were designed to be, not just if your needs are being met. We can't understand your destiny if we don't understand how you were designed.

From that starting point, we move through the equation. Is this kid getting enough sleep? Enough to eat? Enough exercise? Experiencing enough nature? Do they feel safe? We know healthy bodies are necessary to function at our best level, so we embed all this into our education plan by helping our kids self-regulate and pay attention to those things in their life.

We teach them, through daily practice, to pay attention to those pieces so that they grow to be adults who can keep doing that. They need to learn to pay attention to how they feel and to understand the contributing factors that make them feel that way. They need to learn to make decisions about what they need to do to function their best.

[16]Saul Mcleod, "Maslow's Hierarchy of Needs," Simply Psychology, December 29, 2020, https://www.simplypsychology.org/maslow.html.

Things like knowing how to go to God and talk to him. How to breathe. How to get more sleep. How to eat healthy. How to free themselves from anxious or low thoughts. How to break out of spiraling self-focus that leads to depression.

Surprisingly, most kids aren't being shown how to do this. It's not part of our education system. Even while our country has gotten better about destigmatizing mental health issues, we've strangely found ways to mask the actual problems in that process, normalizing it instead of helping kids take ownership of the practices that can help.

Self-awareness is a kind of superpower. If you know the practices, you can self-regulate. If you don't, you're stuck in a fight or flight state. Anxiety makes kids forgetful, and it slows down their thought processes.[17] How can you learn anything like that? Kids have to get their systems into regulation before trying to acquire new information. It's the idea of "Maslow before bloom," where you help students get their physical and emotional needs taken care of before you demand excellence in academics. Flowers don't bloom if they don't have soil, water, and sun.

Finding the Right Hook for Information

My son Mason struggled to learn because of ADHD and other issues. But we discovered that when he was studying for a test, he could remember the information if we taped answers to the wall in different locations. We created anchor points for information so that when he closed his eyes, he could visually see where the information was. Some people know it as a "memory palace,"

[17]Paul, Dr. Sean. "How Does Anxiety Affect Children's Learning?" NowPsych. Dr. Sean Paul, MD, June 21, 2020. https://nowpsych.com/how-does-anxiety-affect-childrens-learning/.

where you associate information with a three-dimensional location, whether the location is in the real world or in your mind.

Associating information with a location isn't just for remembering complex lists. We're in an age of information overload, where we first have to decide what information is valid and necessary before we try to remember it. In the 1990s, author David Shenk outlined some of these problems in his book *Data Smog: Surviving the Information Glut*, making startlingly accurate predictions about how all of us would drown in information if we weren't cautious, needing cues to sift through and find information. What Mason went through happens to a lot of ADHD kids, but in our information-saturated world, where nearly all information is delivered virtually and obtained from the same two-dimensional screens, most of us are in need of retrieval cues for information. We are operating on fewer physical sensory cues to help us remember how we experienced information, experiences we use when it comes time to recall.

Imagine that your brain is a coat closet. When some people open the closet, they naturally pull out a hanger, slide their coat onto it, hook it back on the bar, and close the door. But other people, like those with ADHD or creatives or those with an entrepreneurial spirit, open the closet door and throw their coat on the floor.

When it comes time to retrieve information, the latter group opens their brain's closet door and sees the mess.

"I can't remember!" they think as they look at the jumbled mess on the floor. "I'm so bad at this."

What we do is help kids understand what's happening when their brain dumps information on the floor. If they understand how their brain is working—and we make sure they know that it *is* working, that it's not broken—they can recall information.

I couldn't be doing all that I do on a global level if I was a linear thinker. I'd be completely overwhelmed. I understand the messy closet approach is my own, and I've learned to appreciate the strengths that come from it.

What we do is help kids create hooks to help them remember information.

Let's say I tell you of eleven different objects: tree, light switch, stool, car, glove, gun, heaven, skate, cat, bowling pin, goal post. Then without looking at that written list, I ask you to tell me those objects back to me. Even better, tell them back to me in order.

Good luck. That's a lot of information to remember. You need hooks to hang it on so you can remember it, so let's look at some memory hooks.

Number one is tree. Think of a tree trunk like a number one. Number two is light switch, so think 1-2-1-2 with the motion of turning a light on and off. Number three is stool, so think of a three-legged stool. Number four is car, and you have four tires on a car. Number five is glove, and you have five fingers on a glove. Number six is gun, so think of a six-shooter. Number seven is heaven, and that rhymes. Number eight is skate, and that also rhymes. Number nine is cat, and that has nine lives. Number ten is bowling pin, and there are ten pins. Number eleven is goal post, and the number looks a lot like a goal post.

This is how we teach kids to "hang up" information. Even for people who could do a decent job of getting most of the list items in order, this visual association is helpful. Very few could remember the whole list without this technique.

It doesn't take more time to remember information this way, to hook it. That's the power of really understanding how your brain works and how you connect it to the world. For Mason, anchoring information made the difference. If he could see the picture, he could find the information. But he had to take ownership of the process and be confident of the results.

Where Confidence is Found

Real confidence comes when someone discovers something they're really good at, and they know they can add their unique value to the world. Every kid has unique value. Unfortunately, too many have never discovered it, or we've tried to box it up.

"You can be good at studies," we'll say, cornering A+ kids in their books.

They quickly learn that schoolwork is their lane, not sports. So we end up with the education system we have now where we have distinct lanes: academics, sports, and, at larger schools, music and drama.

Four lanes. Pick one.

Where does this leave you if you're a creator? You start with the premise that you have a divine destiny and are a unique creation. Maybe you're good at several things, but because we pegged you for one lane, you'll never get a chance to practice the other things you would be good at.

Instead, we keep throwing the same things at you in the same way. We'll only let you practice what we think you're good at. Even if you'd be better at music, we'll make you practice harder and harder at what we think you're good at, no matter how frustrating it is for you.

All of this would look very different if we let people figure out how their brains work. If we let them find what they are truly interested in and good at. And if we helped them see and appreciate the abstract qualities of their brain as a gift instead of driving them down a lane where they struggle and think, "I'm just not very smart."

Instead, we have a lot of people walking around thinking they're dumb, comparing how their brain works to someone else and only seeing failure. We suffer a huge loss of human potential because we end up with people who have next to no confidence.

Kids need to be able to walk in confidence, but if they don't understand that their brilliance doesn't have to be the same as someone else's brilliance, they'll never have the courage to lead.

We have brain scans and brain maps of people learning, and so we're able to actually see how brains are functioning. We know which parts of the brain lights up when you have ADHD. We can see short-circuited brain loops in people who have PTSD. We have the ability to connect brain hemispheres that aren't talking to each other. We know that negative thoughts ("I'm bad at math") release corresponding chemicals in the body.

We know this is happening. But instead of responding to scientific discovery, our education system treats everyone the same, completely disregarding this reality. And when they do see inequity, they try to solve it in a backward manner.

In a school system in Oregon, leaders saw that fewer minority kids were taking AP classes. Rather than rethinking the education system that might be feeding that disparity, they chose to get rid of the AP classes. Instead of solving the Maslow needs for specific kids, they limited the potential of others. They ended up doing harm to everyone, which was how they saw fit to level the playing field.

When I was in the Philippines and watched Evangeline walk back to her home among the landfill, I asked myself what *she* needed. Not what two hundred million kids in poverty needed, which would have paralyzed me. No, I asked what one little girl,

Evangline, needed. Focusing on the one child in front of us is the only way it works. We only make real change one child at a time. When we partner with Valor families, we start with that same question: What does your child need for success? We trust God to help us be faithful to serve the one.

Empowering the kids *and* their families to take ownership of the education process is the main thing required to fix education. The system has to be flexible to fit the needs of the individual, and not at some massive, all-encompassing scale. We need to stop thinking in terms of broad "equality" and instead ask what one individual kid needs to succeed. Technology has made it much easier for us to serve the individual as unique and gifted by God.

What if we offered more trade school options? More variety in school? Parent coaching? In Oregon, they didn't define their problem well, and then placed that bad definition on everyone, even casting white kids as the primary problem due to white privilege.

I guarantee you what they'll find is that, even after removing AP classes, white kids will still get better grades in that community. Most of the minority group are Hispanic families where English is the second language. That's tough. The white kids have English as their first language. The school system didn't solve anything. They just saw a statistic they didn't like the look of and exacerbated the problem instead of solving it.

We saw this during the pandemic, when public schools couldn't figure out how to make online education happen despite it being the future of the workforce. This is the education system supposedly preparing kids for that, and they couldn't figure out getting online. They had a whole year and couldn't make it work.

"Not all kids have online access," a teacher told me when we talked about this problem.

We only make real change one child at a time.

Do you understand what they're saying in the name of equality and being fair? If not all kids can have internet access, no kids have internet access. We'll either send homework packets or just do nothing. Some schools stopped grading after kids were sent home because if not all students could access online homework to get grades, no kids got grades for the work they did online.

That's setting the bar for the least common denominator, and that's not how you achieve potential.

In the Philippines, we had initially struggled to serve our students during COVID-19. We asked what we needed to do to get all our students in the village an education. We had to support our teachers better and then send them out of our building to support the community, all the while asking the question: What does this one child need to be successful?

If we could figure out how to get the internet into the bush in the Philippines during the worst of situations, we can figure out how to get it to kids in this country too.

Creating Entrepreneurs

Being an entrepreneur means identifying a problem, then identifying a solution, and then monetizing that solution. I promise that the people I hire are those that fit this description, the ones who offer solutions.

Our education system was built in the nineteenth century, and the goal was to create people who would work in factories or on assembly lines. You wanted people who could follow instructions carefully. We don't live in that era anymore, but we're still educating that way despite having a vastly different workforce and despite what we've come to understand through neuroscience about how our brains function and learn.

The system is broken. We must stop working with what's broken and create what should be.

For me, that translates into purposefully not following any other school on social media. I'm not looking to mimic techniques of a broken system. I've battled with staff about requiring classes on the science of relationships, which they think should be electives because it doesn't fit into our typical education requirements. But because who we surround ourselves with has a tremendous effect on our life, I insist it must be required.

We have to teach what translates into problem solving.

What good is it to teach kids in Haiti to read and write if they can't think creatively and find innovative ways to improve the GDP? They need to be able to see that if there's already ten fish vendors on the street, something else is missing, and it's that something else they need to do.

Entrepreneurs find creative solutions, but our education system doesn't educate for that. We churn out factory workers who do what everyone else does.

Complainers, Critics, and Positioning to Win

After a long, hot day of standing in lines and paying for overpriced tickets and snacks, my family was headed out of a Six Flags amusement park. My son, Mason, was complaining.

"I didn't get to go on my favorite ride a second time because the line was too long!" he whined.

I'm sure every parent has had this moment, where you've tried to make a fun day and all you get from it are complaining kids. It makes you never want to do another fun thing with them again.

I stopped him. "Hey, buddy, what was the best part of your day? When do you think we could come back another time?"

Instead of resolving to never take him to an amusement park again, I took the opportunity to position him for a win. He thought about it, his mind shifting from what he didn't get to what he could get.

"What do you want to see happen?" I asked him again.

"I want to ride that ride again," he said.

"Could you say to me that you want to ride the ride again and ask if we could come back, instead of complaining?" I asked. I'd probably say yes. We had passes.

We have to position ourselves as part of the solution.

Whether it's kids or adults, we have to take responsibility for our lives and learn to state problems in a solutions-oriented way. We have to position ourselves as part of the solution. It takes time. It's practice before it's a habit. Some never accomplish it.

We all know adults who still whine and complain about everything. They're people who we avoid, whether they realize it or not, because their constant complaining is too much to take. The name or face of such a person is probably already coming to mind.

But you and your kids can be different.

You have all the power in the world to position yourselves for favor everywhere by simply seeing everything in terms of potential solutions and potential opportunity. Solutions are boundless if you have eyes to see them.

08

POSITION YOUR KIDS FOR FAVOR

These were desperate parents. Their daughter seemed to be constantly angry for no reason, often focusing her emotions on them. She spent all of her time in her room, isolated and withdrawn, without any explanation. They couldn't figure out what was going on.

Then she went on a missions trip.

After she returned, her parents contacted me. "She's a completely different person," they said. "She's not yelling at us. She's playing her guitar and practicing worship music again. She's actually spending time with the rest of the family!"

This is not an unusual story. I hear this a lot. I'm absolutely convinced of how kids are changed by missions trips. I could tell you stories of kids whose lives did a 180 once they got back home. I've seen kids who struggle with extreme anxiety come back from a missions trip, fresh from having traveled the world, now better able to cope with their first year of college. Kids who worried they were going to end up living with their parents forever come back with confidence in their place in the world. Kids who became active in groups like Habitat for Humanity while in college instead of focusing on themselves. Even kids who turned down college scholarships so they can serve with missions groups instead.

This is what missions trips do when you have missions as a lifestyle rather than just a trip you take.

I know there are some who question the value of sending kids on these trips, wondering if anything changes in the long run. It's easy to simply look at the cost of the trip and wonder if it wouldn't be better just to send that money to a ministry directly. I'm reminded of the disciples who were frustrated that Mary poured such expensive perfume over Jesus's feet, fretting about how that money could have been better used. What's the price tag you put on a life-changing experience for your kid? You can't undervalue the compound effect that experience will have.

Missions trips work. I've seen the results repeated over and over. Missions trips activate the creative mindset and help kids learn their voice. These trips also foster a solutions mindset, which gives kids confidence in many situations. All of it combined helps position kids for favor, putting them in the zone to succeed in a meaningful way for the rest of their lives.

But there has to be more.

We can coach and train them on these things at the school, and they can go on a missions trip that will change them, but at the end of the day, they might still be stuck in a system or situation that's broken. A boat rises and falls according to the water it's on. Maybe that's why some people who experienced a missions trip in their youth view them negatively; they went, had their understanding of the world blasted wide open, but when they got home, they were dumped back into the status quo and expected to function.

What they discovered was never put to work. It just sat there and festered. The goal of changing the world through that missions trip was noble, but they did nothing to make it happen after the jet wheels touched down back home. It was an amazing experience that was never converted into positioning them for favor.

Think of a drug addict who gets out of rehab but doesn't change his environment. He has a relapse. All the hard effort

What's the price tag you put on a life-changing experience for your kid?

goes down the drain because his action (going back to his old environment) didn't line up with his goal (staying clean).

It's easy enough to make goals, but we're not always great at practicing the actions that would get us there. Goals alone don't position your kid for favor.

What Goal Are You Chasing?

The question we have to ask is, What goal are we trying to accomplish? If our goal is to position our kids for favor, what does that look like?

We often hear successful people described as lucky or as some just-add-water instant success. Then we feed that image by only highlighting the pinnacle of what they've achieved. "They had a goal, and look! They achieved it!" It's a false image of what achieving a goal looks like, since a lot of work and positioning goes into their life before they get to that moment of favor.

In our home, our goal was to raise kids who loved Jesus. There was nothing more important, so we looked at the systems that would inform our kids in their worldview.

We weren't into sheltering our kids, which can be a knee-jerk approach to the goal we had in mind and one that doesn't always provide the results you expect. Again, you have to be more intentional about how to really reach the goal and put work into it. We had to understand how our children were being coached and trained and if they were getting opportunities to serve and encounter Jesus. We took notice of what influences surrounded them.

A lot of Christian parents will tell you they have this same goal, and yet they'll still put their kids in the public school system where they're surrounded with things completely antagonistic to their beliefs. And then when Sunday rolls around, the family heads to the lake instead of going to church, unwittingly reinforcing an opposing goal. Maybe the parents don't even have their own personal devotional life at home and aren't modeling other key behaviors associated with people who love Jesus. Yet somehow they think their kids will love Jesus.

You might say you have a goal for your kids, but are you intentionally creating the pathway to it?

Let's say you want your kid to have a good work ethic. Where do they practice that? Or perhaps you want your kids to always do excellent work. Again, are they getting a chance to practice what that looks like?

When I walk into the kitchen at home and see that my daughter has done the dishes as asked but hasn't cleaned the counters, that's not excellent work. I'm not going to yell at her, but I won't let it pass.

> **You might say you have a goal for your kids, but are you intentionally creating the pathway to it?**

"The Taylors have a spirit of excellence," I'll say, pointing out the counters. "We do excellent work." That moment becomes one where she can practice what excellence is.

The issue is that parents and teachers won't have kids practice what they should or even model it for them. Because this is such a common problem, we carve out spaces at our retreats to help families evaluate what their inputs are and what influences are at work in their kids.

Keep in mind this isn't yet another thing the parents can foist off on their kids, it's a partnership. Everyone is involved in creating family creeds, which are statements of understanding that define who you are and what you're about. They are identity statements you can attach behaviors to.

"We are the Taylors. We are an adventurous family," my family's creed says. "We value adventure because it enlarges our perspective constantly. It makes us kick fear in the face."

We are the [your family name]. We are a [quality]
family because [reason].

It's not just about listing the qualities (e.g. "we're a happy family"), but also including why that quality is important to your family.

"We are the Taylors. We value personal health because we believe our bodies are a temple of the Holy Spirit."

Every piece of your creed should have an action or set of behaviors attached to it, something you do that actually demonstrates that value in your family.

What you've done is defined your family's values, and the actions you all take that are based on those values. Decisions become easy because the question is always whether it falls in line with the family creed, no matter if it's about what you'll spend your money on or what activities you'll take part in.

"Mom, I'd like to join this sports team."

It fits our personal health value.

"We have games on Sunday mornings."

That doesn't fit with our focus on Jesus Christ and doesn't fall in line with our family creed. Decision made.

When Elon Musk was asked about how he made decisions in regards to SpaceX, he used this same approach. He said that decisions were easy since his goal with SpaceX was to go to Mars. All he had to do was ask if this new idea would get them to Mars a day earlier. If yes, they'd do it. If not, they wouldn't do it.

Think of Daniel from the Old Testament, who early on was determined to be faithful to God. When a situation popped up that said he would have to either skip praying to God or be killed, his decision was already made. He decided to continue prayer because that was who he was.

This is especially useful when your kids become teenagers.

When they're little, molding consistent behaviors is easier. But when they're older and they're asking to hang out with different friends or take part in different activities, they're going to be angry when you say no. Lines seem blurry, and it's hard to provide a reason for your decision at that moment unless you've decided ahead of time what your family cares most about.

If you have an anchor point like a family creed, you can always stand on that and have clarity about it. We live in a circumstantial world, not a values-driven world. People make decisions based on circumstances instead of values because they hold no absolutes.

Consider how, in the Christian home, the Bible should be valued over opinion.

When I was in college, I had a professor who didn't believe in spanking. He made a great case for his opinion, and I was convinced. When I got home on break, I told my dad that I wasn't going to spank my kids because I didn't think it was right.

"Oh, you value your opinion more than God's on that?" He chuckled.

The world keeps drifting further from biblical values, so you have to get anchored and determine, like Joshua in the Old Testament, who and what you will serve. Otherwise, your whole family will be adrift too.

Being anchored creates stable kids, no matter what happens in their environment. We've moved a lot in our family, but despite that, our kids are very stable. Moving to a different place or situation didn't change our family values.

All of this involves a real level of honesty, of course. You can't state a huge vision for your family, then treat it like some wishful statement you stick to the wall, imagining the day you all wake up perfected. It has to be about behaviors you'll actually practice. If you're not sure how to go about that, a good starting point for your family would be to ask what behaviors you're practicing that you don't like. Or even better, use the blank page approach I've used as a principal. Sit down with your kids and ask everyone what they'd love for their family to be about. What would they like to be true about their family?

For big changes, the behaviors attached to the creed might require habit stacking: starting small with habits that progressively change behavior over time. If you've never attended church, saying you'll attend church every time the doors are open *and* you'll have daily family devotions is setting yourself up for failure.

Start small. Find a church. As habits are created, add another onto it and build toward your goal.

The behaviors and creed might grow and change with your kids over time, making it worth revisiting, but having that document to refer back to is important not just for dealing with your kids, but also to keep you accountable in their eyes.

"I messed up," a parent might say to their kids after doing something that didn't fit the family creed. "I didn't live up to our family values. I'm sorry, guys."

When entire families are transparent about the journey they're making toward the same goal, kids are empowered. They're positioned for favor.

Valor Values

We take this same approach at Valor. We've defined what our values are and make decisions accordingly. One way we have defined our values is with the **Five Cs of Valor**:

1. **Christ-Centered:** *We honor God with our lives and actions.*
2. **Compassion:** *We live with integrity, honor, and kindness.*
3. **Community:** *We value genuine relationships with others.*
4. **Confidence:** *We equip each student in their unique giftings.*
5. **Creator Mindset:** *We are always learning with a growth mindset.*

We absolutely want our kids to be positioned for favor. Sometimes ideas or opportunities come along that, while not necessarily bad, simply don't align with our values. For us, global matters, which encompasses our One-to-One Program. That's our value. As time goes on, the behavior around the values changes and adjusts, but the value doesn't. Valor schools in other countries take on that same value, but they also have things associated with it that matter to the culture they exist in.

Underneath that global umbrella, we have other values we hold to at Valor that position our kids for favor.

YOU ARE NOT A VICTIM

Victimhood is not a value, and it will never position you for favor.

The Five Cs of Valor

1. Christ-Centered:
*We honor God with
our lives and actions.*

2. Compassion:
*We live with integrity, honor,
and kindness.*

3. Community:
*We value genuine relationships
with others.*

4. Confidence:
*We equip each student in their
unique giftings.*

5. Creator Mindset:
*We are always learning
with a growth mindset.*

If I was divinely created for a divine plan and purpose, no one can thwart it. That's a bedrock belief, the one I *must* start from. And if I believe it's true, I must also believe it can be fulfilled. I have to absolutely believe that no one can jack that up, or my theology gets shipwrecked.

Yes, life is incredibly unfair. Some kids are born into situations, either in the home or with other limitations, where they have to ask themselves, "How can I win in this situation?" far more than other kids have to.

But life is working for me, not against me. A lot of times pain points are the catalysts to a prosperous future unless you live in victimhood. If you only focus on how you're a victim, you won't have the courage to step into the next scary space, because you're wasting the time and energy on people who are making life difficult.

Yes, your kid will have teachers and future bosses and people who will mess things up and do things to them that are unfair, and it will seem like setbacks at the time. Accept it. Embrace it. Because your kid can still win and maybe will win *because* of those things.

Valor grew out of a situation like that. There were some very ugly circumstances and people working against what we were trying to build, and it was absolutely unwarranted and unfair. It was public, it was angering, and it was humiliating. I could've focused on being a victim, but if I had, we would've stopped there.

Where focus goes, energy flows.

You put your focus back on yourself as a victim, and the energy stops. You don't go forward.

People who interview for a job at Valor by talking about how bad their previous school was don't incline me toward hiring them. Kids who come into my office blaming a teacher (especially if their parents are with them) will probably get harsher discipline.

If you don't accept personal responsibility, you won't grow. If you don't trust that God is for you even in the midst of unfair circumstances, you won't grow. You won't grow in your faith, maturity, or purpose.

We can empathize and validate the difficulty someone is going through. I'm not advocating cruelty where hurt people are told to cowboy up and walk on broken legs. But we have to find a way to acknowledge what happened without encouraging victimhood. We have to do it in a way that helps someone on the path to a win.

> **If you don't accept personal responsibility, you won't grow. If you don't trust that God is for you even in the midst of unfair circumstances, you won't grow.**

"My math teacher sucks," my son told me as we looked over a test with a poor grade.

"I've heard your math teacher teach, and you're right. She's not great," I said, validating what he was experiencing. "But how can you win?"

Seeing the world through a victorious lens takes training and vigorous effort. Seeing it through a lens of victimhood is our default state. Unfortunately, our culture prefers to set up the scenario as a battle between victor and victim, where there's no justice if everyone wins. Our culture says that if someone is going to win, someone else has to lose.

In a way, victimhood is entitlement, a kind of arrogance that demands more pity, more excuses, more leeway, more exceptions. It's like going to the gym and demanding to be a champion weightlifter while expressing outrage that you'd be expected to lift an ounce. Encouraging victimhood destroys the person who buys into it.

Winning doesn't happen at the expense of another. Winning happens by working hard and serving in humility.

HUMILITY STARTS WITH UNDERSTANDING

Humility starts from the vantage point of seeking to understand the other person's perspective before I defend my own rights. We live in an age where people are keenly aware of being offended and demanding their rights.

At a previous school, a mom burst into my office pointing her finger at me. Her son had been disciplined for some behavior issues.

"You are the most arrogant person I have ever met!" she said, clearly angry. "You are unapproachable. I knew there was something wrong with you since the day I met you!"

Oddly enough, I hadn't met her before. I'd never interacted with her personally at all.

Her outburst could've set the tone for the conversation, and I could've hit back defensively, standing to my feet and justifying why her son was in trouble. I would've been in my rights when faced with such an accusation. But knowing that response would only create a downward spiral, I became conscious of my attitude and body language.

"Help me understand why you feel that way," I said, gently leaning back in my chair to show that I wasn't threatened, nor was I threatening.

Help me understand why you feel that way. That's the response to remember, one you can use when your kids are angry or you're in a confrontation. Unlike telling someone "I'm sorry you feel that way" and dismissing them, you're giving them a chance to explain. It gives you time to think, and it also opens the door to understanding. Seek to understand before you seek to inform.

A soft answer turns away wrath. Humility leads with curiosity.

This approach defuses most confrontational arguments where people come in with all kinds of steam from whatever baggage they're carrying, whether what they're confronting you about is real or imagined.

That mom was taken aback at my response, and she did pause before responding. "I'm not sure what it is," she finally said. "I can't quite put my finger on it, but there's something off about you."

I knew immediately that this was spiritual in nature.

Humility makes room for the Holy Spirit to reveal the spiritual implications in conversations. So much of what is going on is spiritual in nature, having little to do with the actual words or accusations being tossed at you. When we teach our kids about humility and the spiritual implications behind their interactions with others, we are positioning them for favor.

Imagine you walk into a room, and there are two people already there. While the room is silent, you can feel that a big fight has just gone down. It's where we get the saying "you could cut the silence with a knife," because despite the silence, there *is* something tangible there, something you can feel. It's the spiritual nature of what just happened that you're aware of.

I've taught my son, Mason, to read a room before he starts talking for this very reason. He was terrible about barging in and talking, oblivious to what may have happened in a room, and often getting in trouble from teachers who weren't as excited about what he wanted to share at that moment.

"When you walk into a room, pause," we told him. "Take a lay of the land, and get your bearings in the room before you say anything. Be curious first."

We were coaching him and his behavior in line with having humility and spiritual sensitivity, which is one of the ways we positioned him for favor.

RESPECT STARTS WITH EXCELLENCE

People are talking about you, and they're talking about your kids. Are they recommending you to other people or warning them about you? Has your family creed helped create positive talking points or negative ones when it comes to your kids?

One way you position your kids for favor is to teach them to do things with excellence. They can have amazing ideas, have a fun and quirky personality, and be part of incredible innovation, but if they aren't known to do things with excellence, few will want to partner with them. Sloppy work or a lack of follow-through won't rate high in anyone's book.

Being out of position for favor means you miss out. If you don't do things in excellence, I won't introduce you to people who could help you fulfill your dream. If you don't follow through, I'm not going to put my reputation on the line for you and connect you to my network. Excellence matters.

I know of a nice woman whose child is extremely undisciplined. No one wants that kid to come over and visit. No one wants their kid to stay at her house. The mom is oblivious to the reality that her failure to position her child for favor has hurt everyone in that home.

I'm not saying that kids have to be perfect. When kindergartners and their parents come in to be interviewed to go to school,

One way you position your kids for favor is to teach them to do things with excellence.

they're bouncing off the walls. I get it. They're little kids. I'm not watching them; I'm watching the parents. About 70 percent of parents will let their kids interrupt our conversation, will repeatedly say "stop doing that!", will ignore them completely, or will simply hand them their phone to keep them quiet.

The parents who get into Valor are the ones who take a different approach. "Do you mind if we stop for a moment?" they might say to me. "I need to step out for a minute and handle this."

That's a parent positioning their child for favor in that moment at an early age. They are raising kids people want to be around, kids who will have friends, kids capable of self-control and excellence.

Too often parents abdicate their authority, and they look to others to fill that position in their kids' lives. You wouldn't believe how many times parents come to me and ask me to be "the bad guy."

Positioning for favor is an active state. You cannot be passive about it.

"When my kid gets to school, can you take their phone away?" I've been asked.

If you don't want your kid to have a phone at school, don't send them with one. Take it away yourself. I'm never going to assume more authority over a kid than their own parents, and it's when parents are either willing to turn their child over to another to be molded or unaware that they're doing so that we see the problems we have today.

You can't position your kids for favor if you let someone else position them or determine what their values will be. This is something you must do, something God has given to you to do.

Positioning for favor is an active state. You cannot be passive about it. Positioning your kids for favor means every purposeful plan, goal, creed, habit, and action you invest into them is for the sole purpose of creating a human being who can always find the win. We can position our kids for favor in everything, whether that's in the community, in school, with authority figures, with their future spouse—heck, even at the grocery store.

When our kids show up consistently, ready to serve no matter the situation, they are positioned for favor.

09

TRUE FREEDOM

My eyes filled with tears as I listened to this woman's voice, reaching all the way from Australia, telling me of the freedoms they'd lost in just a year's time. She explained how in the midst of it all, her family wanted help getting their kids a good education.

It was early fall of 2021, and we were rounding the corner on a second year of a global pandemic. I'd started the day with a phone call on an encrypted app that was very secure. It had to be; some of the people talking to me were literally risking their lives by having a conversation with an American. I heard a young girl tell me of her best friend's family who was murdered for believing the wrong thing and having the wrong kinds of friends. I listened as families from countries that had once been free spoke of what they'd lost in a year.

"You live in one of the freest places in the world," one woman told me that morning.

I discovered in that moment how much I'd taken my own liberty and freedom for granted. I have a brick-and-mortar campus near Portland, Oregon, and there are restrictions and lockdowns we struggled with. Like many others, I'd felt as if freedom was slipping away, but it took talking with people who literally risked their lives to have a phone call with me to grasp how good I still had it. I'd missed the incredible freedom we had both in Christ and in this nation. And that meant I had a personal responsibility to ask who else needed liberty, and what role I played in providing that.

Taking Freedom for Granted

People remind us that "freedom isn't free" and admonish us not to take our freedom for granted, but what does taking freedom for granted look like? Putting a finger on that seems impossible, but it's actually very easy: we take freedom for granted by using our time in the most useless ways.

I was checked in my spirit when I realized how much time I spent on entertaining myself. How I used the hours and the days and the years indicated the value I placed on freedom. I had the freedom to keep on with my standard career and not go through the work of starting Valor, or I had the freedom to start a school in nations that set kids free, to educate girls in a nation that was literally destroying them.

Yes we have freedom, but how are we using it? How do we leverage it? How do we use it to be a light in this world? You can list all the problems you have in life, all the problems you see around you in your community and nation, but I can promise you there are people in this world who would happily trade places with you and live in your life.

Freedom isn't something that gets put on hold until it's safe to take it out and exercise again. There is no lethargic, hibernating version of freedom. Like a shark that has to keep moving to stay alive, we must always exercise freedom. When we don't, it goes away for good.

During the two years of the pandemic, we hadn't been able to take our kids on missions trips, something we regularly do at Valor. The travel restrictions in place around the world made it difficult, and we'd unconsciously adopted a plan of waiting until things were normal again. Toward the end of 2021, Valor cofounder and friend Doug Wood challenged me about that, asking me when I was going to accept that I had to change the plan, change the way we did things, and stop waiting for things to get back to "normal."

This is the new normal. What we knew isn't coming back. It's our job to look at the new normal handed to us, to stand our ground, and to make sure that freedom is exercised.

"But there's authority over us, and we have to obey that government authority," some might say. It's not easy to determine that moment where the scale tips from obeying authority to allowing freedom to wither, but it's exactly in that moment where freedom has a price.

There are times in history where people have said NO MORE, including in the Scriptures. In the book of Daniel, King Xerxes said no one could pray to any other god but the king. Daniel did not obey, but instead prayed as usual, with his windows open, standing for his conviction and relationship with God. The disciples preached a Gospel that wasn't accepted, that went against the religious leaders of the day.

When we freely exercise the true freedom of Christ, there's a greater opportunity for love.

It's our religious liberties that are the most precious, as so much stems from our ability to live life according to the convictions of our faith. When we freely exercise the true freedom of Christ, there's a greater opportunity for love.

More than once, families of other faiths have come to us wanting to enroll their kids in our school. I don't start with "you have to know Jesus before you can come to this school," but instead, "We love your kids." I take the opportunity to share about Jesus Christ. You would be amazed at the number of times people are surprised that you can choose your faith instead of being born into it. The world is longing for us to step into that freedom from Christ, not just to claim our rights. Where the spirit of the Lord is, there is freedom.[18] True freedom.

How are you using your freedom? How are you exercising it? Are you using your freedom to entertain yourself and grow your wealth? Do you use your freedom to read the Word? I've had conversations with people this past year who were begging for just a page from the Bible. How we stand for liberty today is a spiritual thing, because it is an expression of using the gifts God gave you. Your freedom doesn't come from a politician, but from God.

Think of that family who was murdered because they believed the wrong things and had the wrong friends. If you don't think that can happen where you are, then stay asleep and let the exercise of freedom fall away. That kind of outcome will get to your door soon enough.

Why Freedom is a Core Value

At this point, it should make sense that freedom is a core value at Valor, but it's more than simply waving a flag or creating a slogan. The expression of freedom in education is a reflection of free will.

If free will and choice wasn't so critical in God's economy, he wouldn't have given it to us. Instead of creating automatons who had no choice and did what they were programmed to do, God gave us the opportunity to choose between life and death.

We see this when we go to the Scriptures. Instead of sanitizing stories, we read some salacious details that are a bit shocking. Instead of trying to protect and shelter us from such ideas, God

[18] *2 Corinthians 3:17*

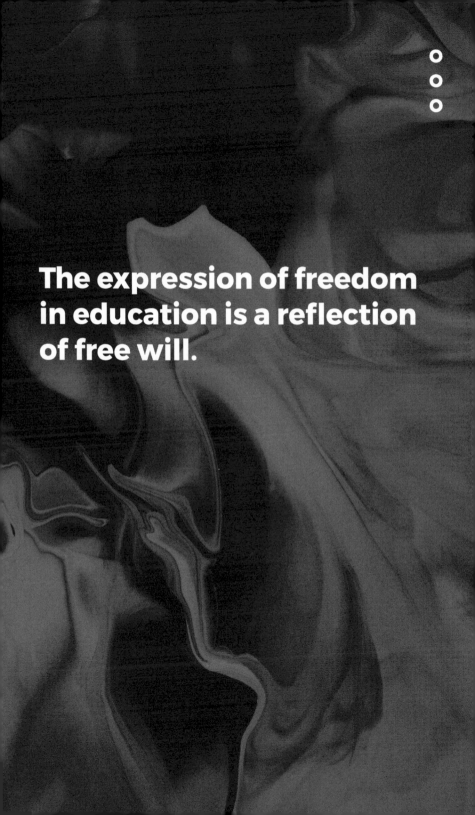

The expression of freedom in education is a reflection of free will.

presents them to us to help us learn as part of the free will process. "Here's where this path will take you," he says. "Which is the better way? Which will you choose?"

From the very beginning in Genesis, God gave us the freedom to choose. In that beautiful garden, God told Adam and Eve everything but one was available to them. "You can have anything and enjoy it all," he said. "But not the fruit of that one tree."

He would have loved to have continued spending time with them and walking with them in the garden, but they chose the one wrong thing. He could have created the garden without the tree of knowledge of good and evil, but he didn't. He gave Adam and Eve the choice of staying in an unbroken relationship with him or not.

"I have come to set you free," Jesus said when he came, thousands of years later, ready to fix that broken relationship. That was the good news, because a desire for freedom is at the core of every human, the longing of our heart.

Freedom is an enigma. It's hard to define, and when you have it, it's hard to grasp. Too often we recognize it best when it's gone. We're able to spot it and talk about it when it's far from us. Freedom requires self-responsibility and thrives best with self-restraint, despite people having very little of either and wanting outside restraint to do the heavy lifting.

Freedom feels unsafe. For example, it seems like a better idea to only allow our kids to learn a limited set of things for their own protection. "There's a huge pit out there, waiting to swallow you up," we essentially say, "but because we don't want you to fall into it, we're not even going to expose you to its existence."

At Valor, I approach freedom by refusing to violate someone's personal agency. That includes not selectively avoiding topics and not deciding for them what they are allowed to know.

We teach students about other religious faiths as well as Christianity, and about both evolution and creation. We don't tell them "it's only this that you should and can learn," but present all the information so they can build an informed understanding and make their own decisions. They have personal agency.

In recent years we've seen the opposite of this concept becoming the norm, and even the disturbing trend of making people think personal agency is a selfish thing. Wear this. Do this. Take this. If you don't, you can't come in, you can't participate, you can't be a part of society. We don't get to decide, because we've accepted the idea that your personal agency infringes on my freedom, and so no one will have either.

Freedom is always on the chopping block, whether we realize it or not. Every generation has something looking to remove freedom, and it's an ever-escalating process that requires us to be aware that it's happening so we can push back on it.

Take critical race theory (CRT), for example. At its heart, CRT is trying to remove the freedom of thought. A white person is an oppressor, and if you don't believe it, you're a bigot. You are not allowed to think critically or question it. You either accept it, or you fulfill it.

Parents want their kids to have personal agency. The younger they are, the fewer choices they get, but as they get older, they need to grow in a direction where they can make correct choices on their own. Anytime we start teaching ideals, we have to use a critical thinking lens. I do this even when teaching scripture, using an apologetics approach to show that you can validate scripture using critical thinking.

Stalin said that ideas were more powerful than guns, so you shouldn't allow your enemy to have ideas. Are we taking a page out of his book by restricting the ideas we'll allow our kids to have? As kids get older, the goal is to teach them to analyze arguments, not memorize conclusions. Too often Christian education has been limited to a mindset of memorizing conclusions and positions, creating a playbook that teaches them what to think instead of how to think. We don't like it when the world does something like that, so we shouldn't take the same approach in educating our kids. The danger of CRT is that it removes the thought and questions from the content.

In a debate, the goal is to win the person, not the argument. If you position yourself as a learner instead of as a judge, you truly exhibit how wisdom creates paths, not positions.

Scripture backs up this approach to free will when it comes to making decisions. You can see how God enabled us to make choices by letting Peter deny Christ three times. God knows the importance of walking through the trials of our bad choices. That's where we develop our faith and thinking.

To be free means to be able to think well. That's why you need to be in a safe environment where you're allowed to ask questions. You have to be able to question the validity of something. When we allow that, we mimic God, because with God, when you genuinely seek truth, you will find Truth. Good questions indicate someone who is really seeking. When students are not curious, we must teach them to be by asking them what they think and why they believe that to be true. Require them to go beyond their opinion.

When you're not allowed to ask questions and are protected from the possibility of coming to the wrong conclusion, the end result can be tragic. This is what I want parents to understand.

I grew up with a brilliant dad who loved science and creation science in particular. Many of our dinner conversations would wrap around the wonder of God in science. Unfortunately, as a child, I wasn't hungry to really understand and evaluate for myself the truths that were generously laid out for me. To this day I regret that I wasn't more curious, because the wisdom my father laid out for me was a gift that took far too long for me to appreciate.

It would have been of great value to me if someone asked what I thought about it all and why. I would have been forced to think critically in those conversations.

My college biology class almost blew me and my faith out of the water. In my Christian school, I was left with the understanding that all evolutionists were idiots, and I was armed with only a few facts under my belt. Just a day or two into class, my hand shot up to challenge the professor.

It's almost painful to think about, even now. I was so ill-prepared for the conversation. I didn't just lack the facts necessary to debate the science or the understanding that people who didn't believe as I did weren't idiots. I also wasn't prepared with good questions. The professor shut me down quickly in front of the whole class with a coherent argument I couldn't respond to.

I nearly lost my faith from that humiliating moment. By the time the end of college rolled around, I had found my legs again, but what if I hadn't? There would be no Valor.

The thing that makes me crazy about Christians is they go after bandwagon items, like Critical Race Theory or Common Core, but they don't understand why they think what they think. Their kids are brought up in this same environment, and when those same kids take that debate to school or the marketplace, they get obliterated. It's at that moment they realize they only believe and know what their parents told them or allowed them to believe, and there's a whole world of really smart people who can make them feel like an idiot.

We always want to vilify people and make them out to be purely evil. But if you talk to people who support CRT, for example, you'll find most of them care deeply about the issues at hand. The value for people is there, and you'll discover some common ground. When we create a group of villains and a group of good guys, our goal is easier: keep the bad guys out, and don't teach your kids anything bad. To be clear, I do not embrace the ideals of CRT or Common Core, but I have studied them and have thought critically about my position on these items.

There are brilliant people on all sides of the equations. You have to ask good questions to find out how they came to their conclusion that is contrary to Truth.

There are brilliant people on all sides of the equations.

I almost walked away from believing God created the universe, not because I wasn't told he did, but because I was *only* told he did. When I came back to my faith a few years later, I took that experience with me. I never wanted another kid to have that moment. I had to teach kids well enough that they understood the reasoning behind the really smart people contradicting what their faith taught them. Like Sun Tzu said in *The Art of War.*

> If you know the enemy and know yourself, you need not fear the result of a hundred battles. If you know yourself but not the enemy, for every victory gained you will also suffer a defeat. If you know neither the enemy nor yourself, you will succumb in every battle.

No parent wants their kid to walk away from the faith and heritage they've taught them, but being afraid to create a safe space to ask challenging questions has that effect. If you think well about your faith, if you ask good questions, if you build bridges with people who hold different ideas, the enemy will hate you for it. They'll do everything they can to destroy your and your kids' faiths.

The best way to prepare for that is to think about a chair. Let's say I have a chair sitting next to me. I point to the chair, and I teach my students about the makeup and quality of the chair. "This is a good chair," I tell my students. "It's very sturdy. It's very trustworthy. It's made of wood, screws, and glue."

The students take notes. They discover what chairs do. They learn all about the history of chairs. They memorize the elements of the chair. They memorize the things you do with a chair. Then they get to college, and a professor looks at them and says, "I wouldn't trust that chair. It's going to break."

Their whole life we've only told them about the chair, and now they're being told that if they sit on that chair and put their full trust in it, it'll break, and they'll end up on the floor, humiliated.

Maybe the chair is *gonna break*, the college student thinks and loses trust in the chair.

But a kid (let's say yours) who has been asked to repeatedly sit on that chair all through elementary and high school, even as they learn all those other things, is in a different position when they get to college.

"Don't sit on that chair! It's going to break."

"No, it's not," your kid says confidently. "This chair has served me many times. I've experienced the strength of the chair. You can't contradict that experience, and I know all the elements that make it strong."

The enemy does great work on kids who have never asked tough questions or been made to sit in the chair. The consistent question at Valor has always been: What does it look like to have kids sit on the chair?

Sitting on the chair for your kids doesn't work. Educators and parents are really good at telling kids things, because it's really easy to fill a kid with knowledge. But the enemy is really good at yanking the chair out from under them, because they don't want them to ever sit down. They don't even want them to think it's possible to sit down.

When you ask your kid to test and walk out their faith in every area of life, including how they think, that's the freedom component. And that's scary for parents because it exceeds their protective space. If you tell kids the chair is trustworthy, but you don't trust it enough to let them sit on it, do you believe what you're telling them?

Kids at Valor learn about other faiths. I'm not afraid to tell them these things, along with the truth, because I really do trust that chair. If I can bring these kids to safely question and understand, they're taking a seat in the chair.

That's why we have an open door at Valor. Nothing gets in front of the cross. You can come to Valor, no matter your faith. You can come believing evolution is true, holding to CRT, and whatever else. We're going to love your kids, and I know the chair will hold.

We often hear that freedom is under assault today, but it always has been. So here is what we hold fast to: true freedom comes through Jesus Christ, and the world will offer up any other version of freedom except the truth. While we prayerfully ask God daily to show us how to exercise freedom and personal agency in our own lives in a God-honoring way, we should also look for an interdependent community that such freedom thrives in, forwarding it to our kids and future generations.

That's the Way of Valor.

Where We Go from Here

Imagine a school where your child's divine destiny was appreciated, where parents and teachers partnered together to raise world changers. Imagine a school that moved students from apathy and complaining to serving and finding solutions.

I started this book by asking you to imagine such a place. You don't have to imagine it anymore because it exists. I've laid it out for you, and while you might not have the entire solution perfectly in your grasp right now, you can see the path to it from where you stand.

What a difference that vision is from what you've known until this moment. Feeling tired, knowing your kids are trapped in a system that isn't working but not knowing what else to do. Feeling angry as you watch amazing kids who are unique in every way limp through a system that sees them as a number to be managed before spitting them out in the world, stripped of potential. You had no voice, your kids had no voice, and there was still so much noise.

It can feel like we're failing our kids, that we're watching their light go out. I've felt that hopelessness as a parent and as an educator. That's the driving reason I pulled the curtain back to reveal what's broken and why.

There are creators in our midst. They are capable of seeing the world as it could be. They're uniquely gifted to create solutions for all those overwhelming problems crushing our world. The question is whether or not you're comfortable living in the broken systems, or if you're serious about encouraging these creators to find solutions.

The question is whether or not you're comfortable living in the broken systems, or if you're serious about encouraging these creators to find solutions.

You could put this book down, recognize there were some good ideas, and go on with your life. Or you can let this book make you uncomfortable, let the ideas grow in your mind, and prod you into action. I'd be disappointed if you were comfortable with what this book had to say, because winning happens outside of comfort zones.

Where you are right now is exactly where you can start positioning your kid for favor.

You can create a family creed.

You can change your expectations for your kids.

You can change where and how your kids are educated.

You can lead your family differently.

You can walk alongside your kids as they move from apathy to impact.

At the end of the day, we all long for greatness in our lives. What will you do before the end of today to make that happen?

Valor is a community engaging in a faith walk around Jericho, believing as we take action on our faith the Lord will deliver this land and all her inhabitants to us. Valor can exist literally anywhere on the earth. We simply need people of faith ready and willing to partner with us to enlarge our tent pegs and build God's kingdom throughout the world.

Acknowledgments

While *The Way of Valor* is a journey about a community reimagining Christian education, it is told from my personal perspective. There were so many critical players who have made this vision a reality and contributed in significant ways. I am sure that this book does not do justice to the important role you have served both in the development of Valor or my life. It is my hope that you would know I honor you for the role you have served. I will be forever grateful for your partnership and support on this journey.

To Lauren, Mason, and Eden, my beautiful children. The way God made you each so unique with your own gifts has taught me so much about how to educate children and call out to their divine destiny.

To my parents Don and Joanne Kopp. Your consistent example of a life of action-oriented faith is the firm foundation that we have built this work upon.

To Doug and Thea Wood, my dear friends and partners in Valor Global Online. You have helped make this book and my dreams a reality. Your courage and generosity have been a constant source of inspiration in my life and on this journey.

To Jeff Ahn and Sarah Byon, my cofounders in Valor Global Foundation. You are such an essential part of my journey and the building of our schools throughout the world.

To Alan and Rashell Linenberger, dear friends who are like family, truth tellers in my life, and my biggest prayer support over the years. I treasure you both—mostly Rashell, but sometimes you too, Alan.

To Jim McKenzie. You have been a voice of wisdom and encouragement, and a champion for me and Valor. I will forever be grateful.

To the original Valor architect team: Holly Neill, Erik Neill, Joey Jenkins, Lamar Hurd, Rashell Linenberger, Alan Linenberger, Tim Black, Kami Naber, Amber McCabe, Katrina Green Jeff Ahn, and Sarah Byon. We have come a long way since the days of writing this vision on my living room windows.

To Pastor Jess Strickland and the Living Hope Board. Thank you for your generosity in opening your doors to this vision. You are an essential part of our origin story, and we are so grateful for You.

To the Valor 2016 staff and our founding families. Thank you for jumping off the ledge with me and walking Jericho. Your courage and willingness to give up your jobs or enroll your children in a school that did not exist will forever amaze me and be a brilliant part of this story.

To the Valor Global Foundation Board: Alan Linenberger, Marshall Bex, Lori Harris, PM Varghese, Jeff Ahn, Sam Sady, and Sarah Byon. Thank you for your service to this vision over the years; only you and God know the countless miracles that had to happen for us to be the vibrant community we are today.

To all those who have served generously on the school board for our brick and mortar campus over the years. Special thank you to Matthew Dodd for your wisdom and leadership of our board.

To our Valor partner school directors: Jane and Justus Amunga (Kenya), Jeong Rye (Philippines), Joey Jenkins (Haiti),

Caleb and Alyssa Mooney (Guatemala). It is an honor to do this work with you.

To the hundreds of Valor staff members throughout the world who have been so important in helping us develop and enact this vision. Your role is so vital in making that vision a reality and I honor you.

To Jordan Loftis and the Story Chorus Team. Your gifts and abilities to tell our story so well is a blessing to us.

About the Author

Angie Taylor believes in disrupting education as we know it and not following the
status quo. Angie cofounded and serves as
the head of Valor Global Online, a digital
learning school which has students in four
countries and thirty-five states. She is also
the cofounder of Valor Global Foundation,
a nonprofit organization which has started

brick-and-mortar schools in the US, South Korea, and the Philip-
pines. Valor Global Foundation provides education scholarships
to students in developing nations.

Angie has been in education, public and private, for
twenty-nine years as both a teacher and a head of school. She is
a published author and a speaker on topics such as school con-
tinuous improvement, teacher development, service-learning
education, and global education initiatives.

Angie holds a master's degree in education, with a special-
ization in technology in education from National University in
San Diego, where she graduated with distinction. She also holds
a bachelor's degree in education from North Central University
in Minneapolis, Minnesota. Angie lives on a ranchette outside of
Dallas, Texas with Adam, her husband of thirty years. They have
three children: Lauren (25), Mason (22), and Eden (16).

About Valor Global Online

Valor Global Online is an online, Christ-centered school that distinguishes itself with daily check-ins that focus on the student as a whole, small classes, an entrepreneurial track, and more. The school was founded in 2017 and is expanding while still maintaining its high-touch, personalized focus. Valor has physical campuses in the US, South Korea, and the Philippines.

Valor Global Online delivers classes in an easy-to-use format that encourages socialization and connection with other students and families. At Valor, we value the whole child and offer physical, emotional, spiritual, and cognitive opportunities. Valor Global Online also offers international study abroad programs, as well as an annual weeklong service trip for high school students. The school is fully accredited with Cognia.

To start your own valor community, reach out to **Valorbuilder@valorschool.org.**

Learn more at **ValorOnline.org.**